The English Text of the Ancrene Riwle

EDITED FROM

BRITISH MUSEUM MS. ROYAL 8 C.I

EARLY ENGLISH TEXT SOCIETY

No. 232

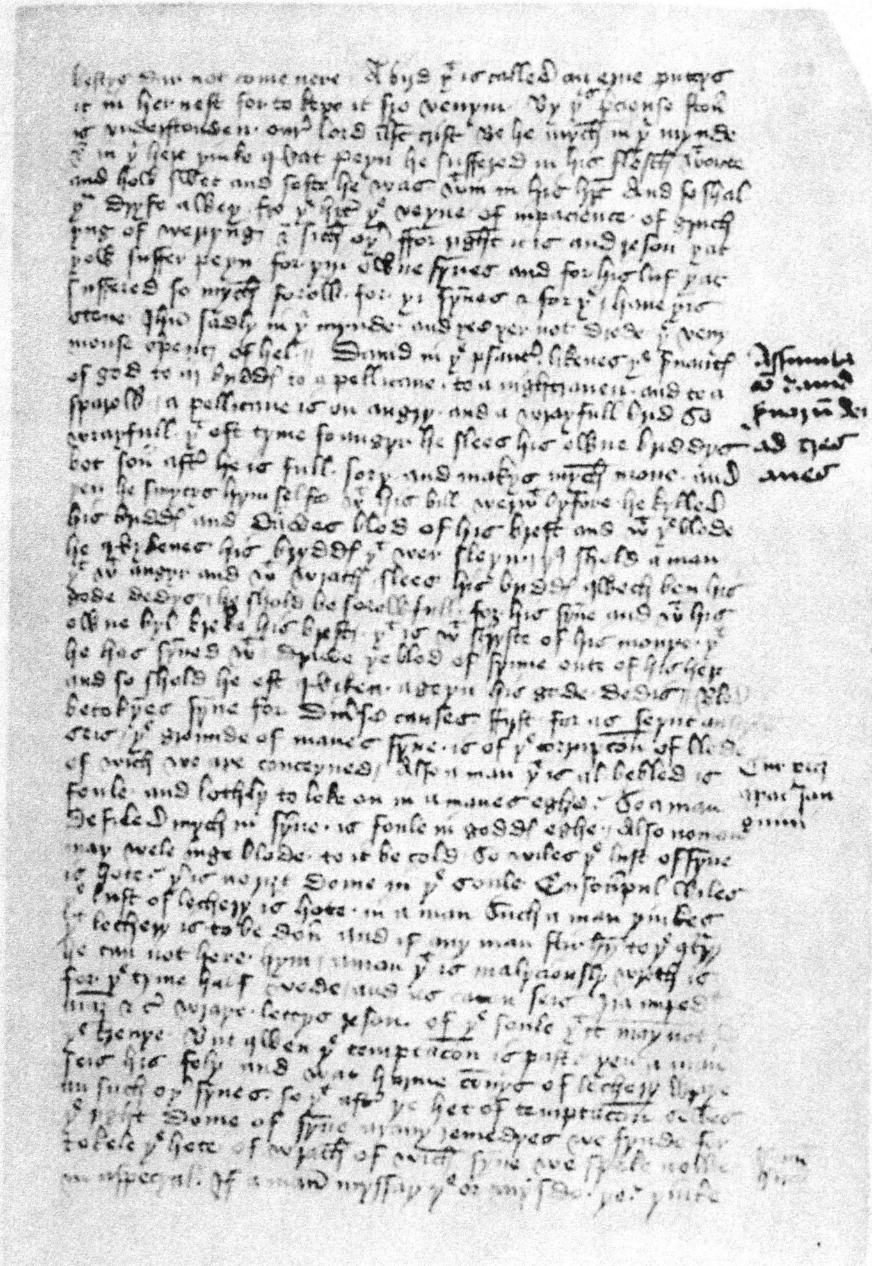

British Museum MS. Royal 8 C. i, f. 133

The English Text of the Ancrene Riwle

EDITED FROM
BRITISH MUSEUM MS. ROYAL 8 C. I

BY

A. C. BAUGH

Published for
THE EARLY ENGLISH TEXT SOCIETY
by the
OXFORD UNIVERSITY PRESS
LONDON NEW YORK TORONTO

OXFORD
UNIVERSITY PRESS

Great Clarendon Street, Oxford OX2 6DP
United Kingdom

Oxford University Press is a department of the University of Oxford.
It furthers the University's objective of excellence in research, scholarship,
and education by publishing worldwide. Oxford is a registered trade mark of
Oxford University Press in the UK and in certain other countries

First Edition published in 1956
Reprinted 1959

Published in the United States of America by Oxford University Press
198 Madison Avenue, New York, NY 10016, United States of America

British Library Cataloguing in Publication Data
Data available

Library of Congress Cataloging in Publication Data
Data available

Original Series, 232

ISBN 978-0-85-991947-0

CONTENTS

PREFATORY NOTE

THE English manuscripts of the *Ancrene Riwle* are reproduced as they stand without emendation. Alterations made by the original scribe are enclosed in obtuse-angled brackets, i.e. ⟨ ⟩; letters or words expuncted are so printed; alterations and additions by other hands are recorded in the footnotes. The capitalization, punctuation, and word-division of the manuscript are retained; the ordinary hyphens used are those of the manuscript, being almost always at line-ends. For a hyphen introduced by the printer where a word has to be broken at the end of a line the symbol ⸗ is used. When a word is divided in the manuscript between two lines and there is no hyphen, a short vertical stroke is inserted in the print at the point of division.

Abbreviations are normally expanded without italics; but ꝥ (for *þet* or *þat*), ⁊, etc. (for 'and' or 'ant'), and abbreviations of uncertain meaning are left unexpanded. If *ƿ* (wyn) is used alongside *w*, it is so printed; but if it is consistently used throughout the manuscript, *w* is used for it.

Mr. N. R. Ker has consented to undertake the general supervision of the palaeographical features of the several manuscripts and has contributed various details to the special descriptions of them.

Members of the Council of the Early English Text Society have seen the volumes in the proof stage and have made contributions towards their revision.

In the present text the letters B and L are used in the footnotes to designate marginal entries in the MS.:

B, a fifteenth-century hand, occurs in the list of contents on the front flyleaf of the manuscript, and on f. 166 (see p. x).

L, a good seventeenth-century hand, has written the words 'Lichfeild tractatus de V. sensibus explicit' on f. 143^{v} (see p. x).

Marginalia not marked with either B or L are, as far as can be determined, in the hand of the main scribe.

The side-notes in this edition are identical with those in the edition of MS. Nero A. xiv.

Letters which are illegible in the original owing to damage to the manuscript are enclosed in square brackets, i.e. [ ].

The looped abbreviation (see Frontispiece) has been expanded throughout as *es*, though the scribe uses *es*, *is*, and *ys* when the suffix is written out.

INTRODUCTION

THE portion of the *Ancrene Riwle* preserved, with omissions and additions, in MS. Royal 8 C. I, ff. 122v–143v, corresponds to Books II and III of the Nero text, long familiar in Morton's edition and now available in the edition of Miss Day for the Society. It is with reasonable appropriateness called in the manuscript a treatise on the five senses. It is not so much a transcription as a free adaptation of the original to a lay audience. The Royal manuscript is of the fifteenth century, of paper except for the flyleaves and with a written space of $7\frac{1}{8}\times4\frac{1}{8}$ inches. It is a collection of theological tracts, some in Latin, some in English. The treatise derived from the *Ancrene Riwle* (art. 5) is written in long lines, about 41 to the page, in a good current hand which appears to be the same as that of the Latin tracts of the Austin friar John Waldeby on the Lord's Prayer, the Ave Maria, and the Creed which precede it (arts. 1–4). Another hand beginning on f. 144 copied a treatise in English on the Seven Deadly Sins elsewhere attributed to Richard Lavenham, Richard II's Carmelite confessor (art. 6). The manuscript belonged to one Hugh Haverel in the sixteenth century and later to John Theyer, with whose collection it came to the Royal Library in about 1678.

Since the name Lichfield occurs in connexion with the paraphrase of the *Ancrene Riwle*, the Warner–Gilson catalogue observes: 'probably by William Lichfield, rector of Allhallows the Great (d. 1447), who is mentioned by Gascoigne (*Liber Veritatum*, *s.v.* Praedicator) as a preacher'.[1] There is nothing improbable about this attribution. Lichfield was well known as a preacher. The London Chronicle for 1446–52 records his death on 26 October 1448 and adds 'the whiche was a good prechour and an holy man þat made in his dayes M^iij^iiij^xx and iij sermones, as it was found in his bokes of his own hande writing'.[2] These have not come down to us, but the sixteenth-

[1] *Catalogue of Western Manuscripts in the Old Royal and King's Collections*, by Sir George F. Warner and Julius P. Gilson (London, 1921), i. 228. The date of Lichfield's death should be 1448. The clue to the identification of the treatise with the *Ancrene Riwle* was given by G. R. Owst, *Preaching in Medieval England* (Cambridge, 1926), p. 111.

[2] Edited by C. L. Kingsford, *English Historical Literature in the Fifteenth Century* (Oxford, 1913); cf. p. 296. The statement is echoed by Stow in his

century catalogue of the library of Syon monastery (as edited by Mary Bateson in 1898) indicates that the monastery had a collection of 'Sermones M. Willelmi Lychfelde'. Lichfield's poem *The Complaint of God to Sinful Man* was popular enough to have been preserved in more than a dozen manuscripts. That a prolific writer of sermons and other religious works should have found in the *Ancrene Riwle* matter suitable to homiletic purposes should therefore cause no surprise.

The attribution, however, rests only on the occurrence of the name Lichfield in the list of contents on the front flyleaf of the manuscript.[1] As the Warner–Gilson catalogue notes, the *Ancrene Riwle* item is here listed as 'optimus tractus de v sensibus secundum lichef[eld][2] destintus in duas partes'. The list was written in the fifteenth century, not much later than the manuscript itself, and it has therefore some value as evidence. It is in the same hand as a good many notes in the margins of the *Ancrene Riwle* and a few notes elsewhere and the whole of f. 166, which contains what is called in the list of contents 'Materia sermonis in die pasce' (art. 12). The price of the manuscript 'xxij s vi d', written on f. 170, is probably also in this hand. The attribution of the paraphrase of the *Ancrene Riwle* to Lichfield caught the attention of a seventeenth-century reader who added the words 'Lichfeild tractatus de V. sensibus explicit' on f. 143v.

Nothing is more certain than that the adaptation of the *Ancrene Riwle* in the Royal manuscript was not intended for hermits or anchoresses. Such an intent would render meaningless the consistent removal of all direct address to the anchoresses in the original and the careful change of those passages in which the anchoress is the person discussed. It is not within the plan of this edition to study the Royal text in relation to other manuscripts of the *Riwle*, nor would such a study be possible until editions of all manuscripts are

Survey of London (ed. Kingsford, Oxford, 1908–27), i. 235, and is hence fairly well known.

[1] The flyleaf is from the commune sanctorum of a Breviary with spaces left for the music. The list of contents has been written in some of these spaces on the verso of the leaf. Dr. Hope Emily Allen has called my attention to this list, and was herself reminded of it by Mr. A. I. Doyle of Downing College, Cambridge, having, as she tells me, missed it in her earlier mention of Lichfield, *M.L.R.* xxiv (1929), 14–15.

[2] The corner of the leaf is here cut away.

available. But two or three examples may be cited to justify the observation just made.

Where in the *Ancrene Riwle* (Nero text, ed. Day, p. 43) the author addresses his 'leoue sustren' and bids them hearken how Christ speaks to the anchoress that ought to be his beloved, the Royal text says 'hear now what our Lord saith to a soul that can find no delight but in earthly things and fleshly lusts'. So in many other passages the anchoress is changed to 'man's soul', as when man's soul, rather than the anchoress, is described as the spouse of God. In a striking passage (Nero, p. 56) it is said that foxes are false anchoresses. The Royal text says that foxes are false men. The Royal text constantly generalizes where the *Riwle* is specific, and is clearly directed toward a more general public.

It would seem to put the least strain upon the evidence to assume for the present that the treatise 'secundum Lichefeld' is by the well-known London preacher.[1]

I have had the pleasure, in the course of a long friendship, of discussing a number of matters touching the *Ancrene Riwle* and the present text with Dr. Hope Emily Allen, always to my profit. I wish also to acknowledge my indebtedness to Dr. Mabel Day, who checked my text with the manuscript and supplied a number of notes on erasures and differences in ink which were not apparent in my photostats.

[1] In this opinion Miss Allen wishes me to say that she concurs. In her article mentioned above she had pointed out one possible indication of the author's special interest in preaching.

ANCRENE RIWLE

MS. Royal 8 C. I

f. 122v (M. 48) Omni custodia serua cor tuum. quia ex ipso vita. procedit prouer .4. With alle warde. kep̄ þin hert for of hit lyfe goþe / þese are þe wordys. of Salomoñ / By þe hert os þe doctor de lira. seyt is vnderstondeñ a. mannes soule. / For. os bodyly mouyng & lyfly felynges proceden fro a mannes fleschly hert.ʼ So fro a sowle. wel dysposed proceden. by grace. meritory dedys of gostely lyuyng / þe v. wyttys of mañ. þat is to sey seyng heryng tastyng smellyng & touchyng are lyke. to v ȝatys by þe wyc̄h is entre. & issu botħ of good & of yuell̄ to þe hert & fro þe hert / Ensoumpul. a man redyng holy bokys / by þat. þat he seth wretyn. conseyueþ in his hert many. blyssed þouȝtes & holy purposes. / Also many tymes. a man seyng his euen cristen in pouert & gret myschef.ʼ is meuyd in his hert / aftere his pouere to releue hem̄ / A man herynng holy ser|monys. is ofte by such herynng stired in his hert to repen|taunce / & gode lyuyng / An ydel. mañ & a curyouse goþe ofte tyme out of his house. for to se or here vanitees / werþoruȝ he is oft stired in his hert to vnclennes. & myc̄h oþer synne / And þus it is of othere wyttes / Seþ not oure lord Matthei 15 þat fro þe hert gon out foule þoghtys. manqwellyng auoutrese. Fornycacions theftes Fals wyttenesynges Wyc̄h synnes defylen a mañ / And þese synnes. are execute by þe instrumentes of þe v wyttis byfore seyd / as by þe handys by þe moutħ & oþer membrys. / Werfor Salomoñ seyng wat profytt commeþ to a mañ. by. wyse kepyng of his hert / and / wat harme commeþ by vn ware kepyng þerof.ʼ Seyth to yc̄h mañ & womañ þese. wordys. byfore wretyn Omni custo|dia &c. / With alle warde. kep̄ þin hert for of it lyfe goþ forþe þe hert is a wyld beste & makyth many a lygħt lepe as seynt gregor se⟨i⟩þ Nichil. corde. fugacius / þat

The heart is guarded by the five senses; the first is sight.

1 .4. *in margin*. B. 31 as *interlined, with caret, after* is. 32 se⟨i⟩þ: i *interlined*.

is Nothyng astertiþ a mañ so soñ as doth his owne hert // Dauid goddes prophet sorowed sum tym þat his hert was astert hym / Cor meum dereliquit me Psalmo 39. My hert he seyd hath forsaken me. And on oþer tym he ioyed þat his hert was commen hom ageyn / Inuenit seruus tuus cor suum 2 Regum 7. / lord he seyd þi seruand hath fonden his hert / qwen so holy a mañ & so wyse lete his hert astert hym.' Sore may we be. aferd. lest oure hertes astert vs And were brake oute þe hert of so holy a prophet.' Certeyn at þe wyndoe of his iȝe qwen he beheld a fayre womañ as /| ȝe shall here aftere / wele & werly f. 123 þerfore. shulde þe wyndow of þe eghe. be kepyd / For not allonly oñ euyll. bot alle euel commeþ of vnwytty lokyng / I preue it is þus. lucifere þorow þat he sawe. & behelde. (M. 52) vnwarly. his owñ fayrnes.' he lep in to pryde. and becam of an aungel. a lothtly deuel. of helle // Of Eue oure first moder /. it is wretyn vidit mulier quod bonum esset lignum ad vestend[um] & pulcrum oculis. aspectuque delectabile & tulit de fructu eius & commedit deditque. viro suo. genesis 3. þat is þus mych to mene. / Eue. behelde þe forbodyn appull. & sawe it was. delectable. to ete. & feyre to þe eghne. and she ete þerof. and gafe þerof to hire husbande. / þus ȝede sight byfore. & mad way to vnlefful / lust of wych folowed. wyked dede. þe peyn werof mankynde now felyth / þis appyll betokynes. alle thyng þat vnleful lust. wych stireþ a mañ to. & delyte of synne. as þus qwen þow mañ lokyst on a womañ werby þu art stired to lechery.' þenne lukist þu on þe appyll / If a mañ had seyd to Eue. qwen she lokyd on þe frute. Eue. Luke not on þe appil. þow castis þin eghe opoñ þi deth / She myght haue answered þus / Sir þe appil þat I loke oñ is forbed me to ete.' bot not to beholde. / Dame Eue (M. 54) haþ many sones & doghteres. þat folowen. here moder / in such answers / Wenest þow sayth sum wylde mañ þat I wyll lep on þis womañ þouȝ I loke opoñ hire / herk. now eue þi moder. lepe after hir eghe sight fro eghe to þe appil. fro þe appil oute of paradyse in to þe erthe. fro þe

Eve sinned through sight.

26 of which folo *crossed out and expuncted after* lust.

erþe in to hel. qwere she ley in presoñ foure þousand ȝere & more. ȝhe. she & hire husband & þe childre þat cam of þam. wyche dyeden. byfor cristes passioun wenten to hel. / lo qwat sorowe cam of vnware sight For os cl'erkes seyn. of a lytel. errour in þe begynnyng commeþ oft mych disese. in þe endyng / Ich feble man. & womañ wel ouȝt þen to drede wen. sche þat was first right gode & wroȝt / by þe hand of god was þorow a sight so begiled & br'oȝt into a brode synne. þat ouer spredyth al þe worlde / Egressa est dina filia iacob. ut videret mulieres &c genesis 34 / Also a mayden. þat hight dina þat was Iacobes douȝter / as it is wre'tyn in genesis. ȝed out to beholde. straunge wemeñ of þe contre þat she was þenne. in / þe scripture seþ not þat she went out for to se men. bot for to se wemeñ / bot wat cam of þat beho'ldyng: She lest hire maydenhed / A prince of þat contrey ra'uysched hir ageyn hir wyl. and few dayes after was þe sam prince

Dinah sinned through sight.

f. 123v & his fader slayne þerfore / þe Burgesis of þe Burgh | þere þey dwelled slayne & þe burgh destroyed Al þis walde þe holy. gost haue wretyn in holy scripture forto warne

(M. 56) men wat harme / þat comeþ of foly sight Also we reden 2 regum 5 þat Barsabee / þe wyf of vry in þat sho vnhiled hire selfe. & waschyd hire ageyn þe soler / of kyng dauid ⟨where⟩ he walked & saw hir so weschyng / sche was occasioñ þat dauid send for hire & synned with hir in aduoutry / Now comeþ forth a mañ ȝong or olde þat holdis hym selfe holy & stronge enogh gostely and hym þink þat he dare boldely stare. & luke vpoñ wemen / It were god þat sych on toke hede. how dauid kyng and prophet of wom god seyd act'. 13. Inueni virum secundum cor meum. þat is I haue found a man after myn owne hert in þe beholdyng of a woman for'ȝate hym selfe & synned in auoutry. & made hire husband vry trayturusly to be slayñ. And þen shold such a foleherdy. wrech be aferde to stare or long to luke on ȝong wemeñ // Also wemen shold take hed þat þe synnes þat dauid did and al þe euyl. þat cam by fornicacion þat was don with dina

Bathsheba made David sin through sight.

24 where *in margin marked to be inserted after* dauid.

Iacobs douȝter þat I spake of cam not for þi þat forseyd wemen̄ Bersabee & dina loked opon men bot for þey vnwarly & vnwyttyly cam in sycħ places. qwer men toke occacion of synne by þe sigh̄t of hem. For þi god com⸗ (M. 58) mownded in þe old lawe exo 21 þat pyttes shold be couered and if any man̄ vncouered a pytte & any best fell into þat pit ⟨he þat vncouered þe pitt shold mak gode for þe best þat fell into þe pit⟩ By þis pittes. are vn⸗derstonden opyn occa'syons. of euyl. As. strump⟨e⟩tes. aray. to gret boldenes on men to stare vpon̄ wemen. or wemen. vpon̄ men̄ / Nyse Iapynges nyse cherynges. & sych othere / Bestes ar bestyal. men. & we'men þat þinken not on þe commoundmentes of god ny lyuen not resonably as men shold do þey þenne þat gyfen occasyons of synne qwerby such. bestly folke synnen. in ded or ellys in wyll consenten to do dedly synne:' þey vnhilen þe pittes and are culpable. of þe gostly detħ of sich bestly peple (M. 60) hound wil in at an opyn dore þer no man werneþ hym

The eyes are the first weapons lechery uses against chastity.

Inpudicus oculus inpu⟨di⟩ci animi est nuncius / augus⸗[tinus] þat mony may not speke for shame:' þe ligh̄t egħ spekytħ it and his arunde berer / of þe liȝt hert þer is sum man þat wold for nothyng / wylne to do fylþ with a wo'man and ȝyt he rouȝt neuer þouȝ sum woman wer temped towerd hym Bot seynt austyn se⟨i⟩þ Non solum appeti sed appeti velle crim'inosum est þat is aman to desire vnlefully or ellys to couet to be so desired boþe ben gret synnes. as a man fiȝtys with iij maner wepynes. with arowes. & dartys schotyng on far / with spers more. nyȝe & with swerdes & knyfes. most nyre / þus weri⟨i⟩þ le'chery ageyn chastite þat is godes spouses First he schotys þe arowes /| of liȝt egħ þat flyen lightly as. f. 124 federed. boltys. and wonden þe hert he fightes as. with a spere. mor. nere qwen. he stireþ to lechery by vnclene. & flateryng / wordes / Swerdis dynt is foule hand'yllyng /

7–8 he . . . pit *inserted in margin, with caret.* 9 strump⟨e⟩tes: e *interlined.* 17 a *interlined after* peple. B. 19 inpu⟨di⟩ci: di *interlined.* 24 se⟨i⟩þ: i *interlined.* 28 sagitte lancee & [glad]ii *in margin.* B. 29 weri⟨i⟩þ: i *interlined.*

lusty kyssyng & þe foule dede / woso þerfor. is wyse be (M. 62) ware fyrst of þe schote of þe egh̄ // Were not he to moch folehardy þat wold b⟨o⟩ldly holde forþe his hede in a open kyr.ˈnel.·/ wyles men withoutforth with qwareles. aseyled þe castel. / þe kyrneles of þe castel. of þe soule are þe eghne. Forþi euery man & woman be war / how he lok⟨i⟩þ.·/ For. þe weriour of hel. is redy to schot wiked stirynges of synne by þe eghsiȝt Bernardus sicut mors per peccatum in orbem.·/ Ita per has fenestras intrat in mentem Seynt Bernard seiþ as deth cam in to þe world þorow synne.·/ So þorow þe eghen deth̄ haþ entre in to þe soule Lorde how besy wold men̄ be. to stop̄ ich hole of hire house & þey wyst þat þay myȝt þerby schitt oute bodyly deth̄.·/ Mych more. besy shold man be. to kep̄ wel. his egh̄ sight̄ & his oþer wyttys. þat gostly deth entryd not by hem / Al holy wrˈytt is ful. of wernyng / of kepyng / of þe egh̄ Psalmus 118 Auerte oculos meos. ne videant vanitatem. lord seiþ dauid turne away myn eghen þat þey se not þe worldes vanite Iob 31 Pepigi fedus cum oculis meis ut non cogitarem de virgine I haue mad a couenant seiþ Iob with myn eghen. þat I shold not þink. on a virgyn Iob seyd fule wele for after þe egh comeþ ⟨þe⟩ þouȝt and after þe þouȝt comeþ þe dede þis (M. 64) wyst wele Ieremy þat mournyngly seyd oculus meus depredatus est animam meam tre 3 þat is to mene Weiylawey myn egh haþ robed my soule Wen godis prophet mad sich mone of his egh̄ mich more ouȝt many man & woman to sorow for. wykednes. þat þay haue. don̄ þorow þayre egh̄siȝt þe wysman askyth ecclesiastici 31 wethere any þing harmeþ a man more þen doiþ his egh̄ Oculo quid nequius. totam faciem lacrimarum Al þe face he seiþ ⟨sal⟩ be wet with teres for þe siȝt of þe egh̄ þus mych̄ is seyd of þis wytt / & mor. shal be seyd after þerof // heryng is þe secund witt þat shold. warly be

3 b⟨o⟩ldly: o *interlined.* 7 lok⟨i⟩þ: i *interlined.* 21 þ *crossed out after* shold. 23 þe *interlined*; 3 *crossed out after* þe (1). 25 tre *sic for* treni. 32 sal *interlined with stroke.* 34 Auditus *in margin.*

The second sense is hearing; under it I will treat first of speech.

kepped Bot for hering & spekyng goñ togeder:ʹ it is to speke of hem ij togeder to speke mycħ with vnclene or harmeful. peple. is but foly by þe wey of company or comyn dalyanse / Eue oure oldest moder in paradise held (M. 66) long tale with þe eddre & told hym qwat god had seyd to hire & to hire husband of etyng of þe apple & by hire talkyng þe fend vnderstod hire febylnes. & hire vnstabilnes. & fond þerby a way to bryng | hir to f. 124v confusion Oure lady seynt mary did on an othere wyse sche. tolde þe aungel. no tale bot asked. hym discretly. þing þat she knew not hir self / Folow þerfor oure lady. in discret spekyng & heryng & not cakelinge eue þat botħ spake. & herd vnwisely haue ȝe not þe kynde of an henne. / an hen qwen sche haþ laid an ege. scho can but cakyl. & qwat comeþ þerof:ʹ Comeþ on & takeþ hir he'rne a way. & oft etiþ hem of wich sche myȝt haue broȝt fortħ qw'yke byrdes & gode / þus þe fend liges in wait wen men & we'men. doñ wele. or seyn wele. wycħ wordes or. dedes if þay wer wisely contynewed / shold be os bryddes styyng vp̄ to heuen And wat tym þay bosten of hire gode dedys or fallen in to vayn talkynges with veyn cumpany þay lese of tyme by mycħ specħ & vn- prophetable. talkyng gode wordes & dedis byfor doñ and þe Fende deuoures þat þat frute shold com̄ of // A pore peddie makiþ oftmore noise to sel. his sop̄ & his nedyłł þan doiþe þe rycħ marchaunte. with al his dere worþi ware þus þay. þat do but lityl. gode spekyn mycħ mor

Shun all idle talk.

þerof þen men of gret vertue doñ of hir god dedis // Micħ (M. 70) foole wer he þat myȝt chese qweþer he wolde grynd wete or chaf to his profyt:ʹ If he wold chese to grynd þe chaf:ʹ þe ouer party & þe neþer party of þe mouþ are like ij gryndyngstonys. of a mylne þe tonge is þe clap̄ holy wordys & profitable are like to wete // vayn wordes & vnprofitable ar likened to chaf / For bestys as ar fed

8 Eua *in margin*. 11 Maria *in margin*. 15 Gallina *in margin*. 25 peddie *crossed out and* peddelere *interlined*. B. Exemplum de riuolo *in margin*. 31 Os comparatur molendino *in margin*. 34 as *interlined after* For, *with stroke*. B; as *struck out*.

with chaf:ʼ so bestely men delyten hem. in such veyn. & vnprofita|ble. iangylyng loke þen þat ȝoure mouthes grynd wordys of soul hele. & no wiked wordys. // If þer com̄ euyl tales or euil tiþinges to ȝour eeris wary ȝe not. (M. 72) curse ȝe not ny sweriþ ȝe not veynly. spekiþ no ry- bowdry. lo qwat Seneca seiþ Ad sum|mam volo vos esse rariloquos. & pauciloquos. I wyl he seiþ þat ȝe take þis for. a reule þat ȝe speke seldom̄ & lityl Mich̄ peple þat ar bonden to cylence as religyouse folke. ankyres & ankereses / ar like to floode ȝatys. of a mylne wych̄ long tym̄ withstandiþ þe water & kepiþ it þat it flow not / Bot wen þe flowdeȝatys ar opened. þen shotys þe watir oute at onys / þus many such̄ peple. kepyn silence for a tym̄ in certen places. But wen þe place. & occacion of spekyng:ʼ þen þay speke to mych̄ & veyn þus did þe frendis of Iob. þat were commen̄ to comfort hym þay sate still vij dayes. But wen þay begunnen to speke þay couþe not stynt her tonges / Sent gregory seiþ Iuge silencium cogit celestia metitari / longe silence he seiþ gadiriþ þe þouȝt to heuenward As ȝe mow sè þe watir wen men stoppyn it þat it may not renne dounwarde:ʼ f. 125 þen it strechiþ vpwarde þus stoppys ȝour /| wordys þat commen of veyn þouȝtys:ʼ & þen wil not ȝoure wordys ny ȝour þoughtes. flete al aboute þe world / as don̄ þe wordis of gret Iangilers & mych cakilers. wen ȝow most nede speke. a li|tyl. lifte vp̄ þe flodeȝate. of ȝoure mouþ as men don̄ at þe mylne. & lettiþ it son̄ doune. ageyn. (M. 74) Mo sleiþ. worde. þen swe-rde. / Mors & vita in manibus. lingue prouerbiorum 18 / þat is lyfe. & deth̄ are in þe handes of þe tonge. Qui custodit os. suum. custodit animam suam Prouerbiorum 21 wo so kepiþ. wel his mouþe:ʼ he kepiþ his soule. Sicut v⟨r⟩bs patens &c þat is to mene. he þat can not kep̄ his tonge fro ka|rpyng:ʼ he is as a cyte withowten̄ wal. þat ich̄ þing /

Speak as little as possible.

9 Exemplum de Flodȝates *in margin*. 10 Religious mens silence *in margin*. L. 15 comit *interlined after* spekyng. B. 17 De silencio *in margin*. 32 v⟨r⟩bs: r *interlined*. *Space for 4 or 5 letters after* &c.

may entre in to. // In vitis patrum it is wretyn. þat on preised diuerse men of gode conuersacion to an holy fadire and he answered / Boni vtique sunt sed. habitacio eorum non habet ianuam. quicumque vult intrat & soluit asinum Godehe. seyd þay beñ bot hire wonyng haþ no ȝate. here mouþes are. full of wordes. wo so wil. may go in & lede forþ here asse þat is her vnwyse soule. For þi seiþ seynt Iam̃e. iacopus Si quis putat se religiosum. esse non refrenans linguam suam sed seducens cor suum huius vana est religio þat is if any mañ wene þat he is religious. & brideles not his tong:' he begyleþ his hert his religion is vayn / þe brydil is not al one in þe hors mouþe but it settiþ aboute his eghen. & goiþ aboute his eiers for al thre haf mych nede to be. brydeled. bot in mouþe sitteþ þe iren & on þe liȝt tong for þere is most nede. For wen þe tong renn⟨i⟩þ in a tale it is loth to stinte / Oft we þinken wen. we begyn to speke:' to speke. lityl & wel. to sett oure wordes:' but þe tong is sleper for he wadiþ in wete & slideþ lightly fro a litel word in to ma'ny. & þen as þe scripture seiþ. in multiloquio non deest peccatum / Mich̄ pepyl. begynne it neuer so wel. shal not fayl of synne For fro trew spekyng. it slideþ oft to fals / Fro gode. & holy spech̄:' to yuel & wanton. Fro mesure ⟨in⟩ to out of mesure / Fro a drop̄ in to a gret flode. þat drenchyth þe soul. For with þe fleting worde. (M. 76) fletiþ þe hert:' So þat long after it is not gedired. wel togedir Et os nostrum tanto est deo longinquum quanto mundo proximum &c / Seynt gregor seiþ in his dialoges / þe more nyȝ þat oure mouþ is to wa'rldly spech̄:' þe ferþere it is fro god / Oure lady seyn mary þat ouȝt to al men to be ensaumple:' was. of so litel spech̄ þat nowere in þe gospel. we fynden of hir spech̄ bot iiij tym̃es & þo were wordes of gret discrecion & gre⟨te⟩ myght̄ / First she spake with ⟨þe⟩ aungel gabriel. / luce 1º Of þe wich̄

Our Lady spoke seldom, but her words had power.

10 Exemplum de freno *in margin.* 16 renn⟨i⟩þ: i *interlined.* 19 þ *interlined after* for. 24 in *interlined.* 32 1ª De loquela marie *in margin,* 1ª *and* marie *being written by* B. 33 gre⟨te⟩: te *interlined with caret.* 34 þe *interlined with caret.*

spekiþ seiþ seynt Bernerd to oure lady In sempiterno Dei verbo facti sumus omnes & ecce morimur In tuo f. 125^{v} breui responso reficiendi suus vt ad vitam | reuocemur responde verbum & suscipe verbum profer tuum & suscipe concipe Diuinum. Lady he seiþ by þ^{e} endeles worde of god we al wer made Bot þorow oure synne we dyen. / In þ^{i} schort answere we ben to be reformed þat we be called agayn to lif answer a word profir þ^{i} worde & conseyf goddes worde. For wen she seyd ecce ancilla domini &c loo here þ^{e} hande mayden of þe lord Be it doñ to me after þ^{i} worde. At þ^{is} worde goddys soñ & soiþfast god bicam man & þ^{e} lorde. þ^{e} wyc̄h al þ^{e} warld myȝt not comprehend bischit hym in þ^{e} maydenes. (M. 78) wombe // hire secund spekyng was with Elizabeth moyder of seynt Iohn̄ baptist & þere she mad þ^{is} can'ticle Magnificat & þere she spake þ^{e} lengest for in þat ympne she preised / & magnified god. // þ^{e} thryd tyme she spake at þ^{e} weddynges. wer wyne fayled. werafter hire word crist tur'ned water in to wyñ // þ^{e} iiij tyme. was she myst hir soñ & eft founden hym. and wondre folowed hir wordys þenne:' all myȝty god bowed so lowe þat he becam̄ soget to a pore mañ & his wyf Ioseph & mary / Takiþ hede. & lerne herby how. seldom spech haþ gret strengh̄ vir linguosus non dirigetur in terra / a man ful of wordys. seiþ dauid sal not lede right life in erþe For þ^{i} he seys. dixi custodiam vias meas. ut non delinquam in lingua mea ypalage. as if he seyd I wil kep̄ my tong. þat I trespas not in my ways. For and I kep̄ wel my tong:' I may wele hold þ^{e} wey^{e}s to heuen For as ysay seiþ Cultus iusticie silencium Isai þe tiling of rigt̄hwisnes is silence / Silence tilieþ. rightwisnes. & rightwisnes. wel tiled bry'ngeþ forth soul fode. for rightwysnes is vndedly as þ^{e} wysmañ seiþ. iusticia immortalis est Isa ioyneþ silence & hop̄ togedir & seiþ þat in hem standiþ gostly

From silence springs hope.

3 suus *sic for* sumus. 8 & take þ^{e} worde *in margin marked with stroke to be inserted after* word. 14 2ª loquela sancte marie *in margin*. B. 17 3ª loquela sancte marie *in margin*. B. 19 4^{a} loquela *in margin*. B. 24 dirigetur *followed by* dirigetur *crossed out*. 33 *Space for about 5 letters after* est

strenght In silencio & spe erit fortitu'do vestra isai & takiþ now hed wy he seyd so for wo so is mych still. & kepiþ long silence:' he dispoysiþ hym selfe to speke warly. & to wyrke auisely and to ware spekyng & auisily wy'rkyng is hop̄ ri3tly ioned / For as yuel spekyng & wiked wyr'kyng stiren a man to wanhop̄:' So wyse. & seldom spekyng with gode wirkyng stiren a man to trew hop̄ quia spes est certa exspec'tacio future bea[ti]tudinis ex gratia & meritis proueniens. hope is a certeyn abidyng of blis þat is to com̄ wich̄ certeyn abydyng cummeþ of grace & meritis / hope is a certeyn abidyng of blys swet spice within þe hert þat m⟨a⟩kiþ swet al þe bitter aduersite (M. 80) þat þe body drynkiþ And wo so cheweþ spise:' it were gode he held his mouþe to geder þat þe swete breth of þe spices & þe strenght belef with hym in þus a vertuose man shuld hold his lipes to geder not commendyng hym selfe neþer shewyng oute his wisdam vnwarly. neþer vse /| mych commyn carpyng. lest his hop̄ lessid þerby:' chew f. 126 in his mynd by holy meditacions þe godnes. & þe kyndnes. þat god haþ showed to hym. his own synnes his perelles. compassyon̄ on̄ þe peple þinke oft on þe pay'nes of hell. & of þe blisse of heuen & speke litel. with men. bot as ned and profit asken. & micle. with gode. And þus shal amannes hop̄ þrow silence be strenghted. and as

Listen to no evil speech.

towching 3oure heryng kepyth it wel and heriþ not 3our thankys. ydel spech. foule spech̄ neþer wyked spech̄ Idel speche is yuel. Foul spech̄. is wors. / wiked spech (M. 82) is worst / Idel it is & no3t / al þat no god comeþ of and of ich such̄e idel worde shal men 3eld rekynyng at þe last dom̄ de omni verbo ocioso &c Matthei 12 Rekynyng shal be made þere wi ydel wo'rdis are spokyn & whi men haue delyte to here hem // Foule speche is of lechiry & rydbaudly fro wich maner of spech̄ men sholde stop̄ both hire mouþes. & heers for gret hermes þereof.

1 *Space for about* 4 *letters after* isai. 12 m⟨a⟩kiþ: a, *perhaps by scribe, interlined above* er, *stroke through descender of* r. 34 heers: *second* e *altered to* r, *and* r *struck out, also* ers *expuncted.* þat comit *interlined after* hermes. eres *in margin*. B.

Wiked speche & venymous:ʼ is heresi lesinges. Bakbytyng fla'teryng / heresi. is fals. Doctryne. contrary to holy scriptur / obstinatly defendid / lesyng is so yuel os seynt austyn seyiþ. þat for to shilde þ^{i} fader fro þ^{e} deth þow shodest not lyȝe God seiþ þat he his selfe is trewþe and wat is more contrary to treuþe þen lesyng / Crist seiþ Ioannis Diabolus est mendax & pater eius / þ^{e} deuel is a lier and fader of lesynges / For þ^{i} ich̄ man & woman þat stiren her tonges in lesynges:ʼ make of her tong a cradil to þ^{e} deuyles childe & rok-yn hym as his norys. / Bakbytyng. flateryng and eggyng to do yuel:ʼ is not manes speche bot þ^{e} deuyles langage & þ^{e} deuil bygan hem in paradyse wen he lied opon god & ba'kbited hym. to eue þ^{e} first woman and flatered hir & egged hir to breke þ^{e} forbode of god genesis 2 þ^{e} scripture seiþ Si mordeat serpens in silencio nihil minus habet eo qui detrahit in occulto / þat is to mene þat a bakebiter wich̄ is þ^{e} eddir kyndelyn wen he bakbytiþ priuely is

(M. 84) no better þen a serpent þat stingiþ preuely. for þe bakbyter / as an eddre. beriþ venom̄ in his tonge. þ^{e} flaterer blyndiþ men & putteþ prikes in her eghen. / Gregorius adulator ei cum quo sermonem. conserit quasi clauum in oculo figit Ecclesiastici þ^{e} scriptur seiþ Noli esse in conuiuiis eorum qui conferunt carnes a vescendum þ^{e} bakbiter chewiþ manes. flesch on þ^{e} friday & pekkiþ with his blake byl̄l on qwike men. bothe gode. & badde / as he þat is þ^{e} deuyles ra-vyne of hell. wold he pike & tere with his byl̄l stinkyng rotyn flesch̄ as is rauenes kynde þat is wolde he sey yuel by no other bot by hem þat rotyn & stynken in filthy synne:ʼ ȝitt were lesse wondre But he pikeþ with bakebityng. holy peple wych̄ lifen in god / þis ij wrechys. Bakbiters. & flaterers. are þ^{e} deuelys gongmen / foul it is to speke bot foulere it is to be sych̄ bro'theles. / þ^{e} flaterer office is to hil and to

Backbiting and flattery are inspired by the devil.

Backbiters.

7 *Space after* Ioannis *for chapter number.* 15 *Space after* seiþ *for about* 4 *letters.* 23 *Space left after* Ecclesiastici *for reference. This should be* proverbiorum 23. 25 *Erasure of about* 3 *letters after* chewiþ. 30 detractor & adulator *in margin.*

couer þe fendis gonge And | þat he doiþ as oft as he with f. 126v his fykil flateryng glosiþ aman in his synne & so hiteþ it with his fagynge þat he þat doiþ þe synne feleþ not þe stynke of his owne synne. wich stenkiþ most foule. to god & to al. gode. men. / þe bakebyter vnhileþ. it & vncouereþ þe fendys. gonge. & opeñ synne so wyde. þat it stinkeþ to soure / ȝhe oft tym synne þat was hid & preuey. þes ij maner of wreches. ben euer besy in þis foule ocupacioñ þat boþ þe bakebiter. & þe flaterer / stynken of hire euyl. besynes. & bryngen ich sted in stinke. were so euer þey commen / Flaterers are in þre (M. 86) maneris. þe first are euyl. / þe secunde are wers / þe thed are we'rst þe first maner of flateryng / is þis to preis a gode mañ in his pres'ens. wich makiþ hym to wene þat he is better þan he is / And if He sey wel. or do wel:' þe flaterer lifteþ hym Vp̄ to hy & gyfeþ hym occacion of depe fallyng / Ve illis qui ponunt puluillos &c ezechielis 13 // þe secund maner flatering is þis If aman is yuel & seiþ & doiþ yuel. þat is synne. is so euil þat it may on no wise be ageyn'seyde:' þe flaterer. se⟨i⟩þ it is not so yuel as men maken it þow art neþere þe first ny þe last þat haues doñ þus þow hast many felowes. let god alon man þu go⟨i⟩st not alon Many oñ doiþ wele worse // þe þryde maner flaterer. is þe werst for he preiseþ a man in his wikednes. as þay þat sey to a knyȝt þat pileþ his bondemen A sir þou doest wele. Laudatur peccator in desi'derijs anime sue. &c Psalmus For euer men shal. pluke. & pile þe chorle For he fareþ as doþ þe wyþeg þat springeþ & spredeþ þe better þat men croppen it oft augustinus adulantium lingue. alligant homines in pec-catis þe tonges of flaterers bynden men in synes / þus þes flaterers hilen þe filth of synne. þat þe doors of synne felen not þe stinke þerof for. if þey did:' þey wold wayt it & shune it // Clemens homicidarum duo sunt genera.

Flatterers.

The backbiter described.

1 dont *altered to* doiþ. 3 fagynge *crossed out and* flatryng *interlined*. B. 8 De mendacio detraccione & advlacione *in margin*. 13 thed: r *interlined after* h *in later hand*. 14 Tres species adulatorum *in margin*. B. 20 se⟨i⟩þ: i *interlined*. 23 go⟨i⟩st: i *interlined*. 28 wyþeg: i *interlined after* e, *and* g *altered to* s. B.

qui corporaliter occidit & qui detrahit &c þere are ij maner bakebiters þe first is yuel þe se|cund is þe wars. (M. 85) þe first seiþ openly euil. by anoþer & spekiþ oute all his atter / & al his venom. all þat comm⟨e⟩þ to mouþe // þe secund commeþ forþe. & as. he were a mannes. frende. he casteþ doune his hede. & begynes to syke. & make heuy chere Welaway he seiþ & wo is me þat he. or she haþe doñ so euil. I warned hym before. þat here synes. wolde com̃ oute bot my counsel helped not It shold neuer haue ben wryed for. me. Bot now. it is so wide knowen. þat it may not be hidde yuel men seyn it is & ȝit ⟨it⟩ is wel wors. In many oþer þinges he or. she is to lufe bot in þis defoute. I am sory I shall sey it he or she is mych̄ to blame þese ben þe eddre kyndli|nges of þe fend of hel. þat Salomon spake of God graunt / we (M. 92) kepe oure eers. fro sich venomose tales A cristen manes hert howiþ to be þe chaumber of allmyȝty god þis latin //| f. 127 worde cor þat betokyneþ a hert in englich̄. haþ iij letteris. C & O & R C. for camera. þat is chaumbur. O for omnipotentis þat is almyghty R for regis / þat is of a kyng So þat cor. þat is to mene manes hert scholde. be þe chaumbre of þe kyng almyghty / wele þene shold þe wittys. wych̄ are entrees. to þis chaumbre. be keped Fo⟨r⟩ þer commeþ neuer noise. ny non synne. to þe hert. bot if it com in sum maner oþer by þe eghe. by þe eer or. by sum oþer membre. of þe wyttys. and þe more þat þe wittys. ar spred outwarde.⸍ þe lesse. gostly felyng haþ þe hert inward. For þe more þat þe egh̄ totiþ owutward.⸍ þe lesse gostely brightnes. of oure lord reseyuiþ þe hert inward / Qui exteriori oculo necligenter vtitur.⸍ iusto dei iudicio interius excecatur /. Seynt gregor. seiþ wo so vsiþ necli|gently his vtter eghene.⸍ by þe right dome of god he is blynd withineforth þat he may not se god and þe godnes of god as hym behoued. & so he lufes god mych þe lesse / For gret knowyng of

1 due species detractorum *in margin*. B. 3 *crossed through after* are. 4 comm⟨e⟩þ: e *interlined*. 12 it *interlined with caret*. 16 eers: i *interlined after* r. 24 Fo⟨r⟩: r *interlined*.

god is gret help. to lufe god mych We rede genesis 27 þat þe owtward eghen of ysaak derked. & he myȝt not se. / Also holy toby was blynd tobie 2 But gret gostly. & inward sight. had þey boþe. þus. be ȝe as blynde. to behold thynges ow⟨t⟩ward vnprofetable. / And god wil gif ȝow inwa'rde. light as he gafe hem. to know godes godnes. & so to luf hym þen sal ȝe se how. þe wold is noght or. lytyl. worth Wat foly it is to set ȝoure luf on warldly þing / ȝe shall se þe fendis wiles. & his diceytes ȝe shal fele in ȝour selfe remorse. and byttyng of conscience. & how ȝour synne harmeþ ȝow. ȝe shal consider þe hydouse peynes. of hell þat wychid folke deseruen. & per chaunce. ȝe haue deserued þat shal meue ȝow to penaunce. ȝe shall þinke on þe dredfull houre. of ȝour Deth Also. of þe swet blyses. of heuen how ich man & woman. þere shal. know oþer / þer shal ȝe se oure lady. aungell & also seyntes & souerenly þe blissed Trinite. Fader & son (M. 94) & þe holy gost / þer is our kynd in iesu criste. & his moder abuf al aungell Ich cristen man oight to know. þat is no worldly siȝte. ny worldly heryng neþer worldly talkyng so swete. & so delicyouse:' as is to þinke to speke. & to here such. gostly. materes. hoc est manna absconditum quod nemo scit nisi qui accipit apocalypsis 2 þat is to mene. þat þe swetnes & þe in ward sight and meditacions þe ioyful. herynges & talkynges of sich gostly. & heuenly maters. ben hid alway & spirituel gladnes þat noman knoweþ:' bot he þat haþ tasted & þis tast sendiþ god to hem þat fliȝen. worldly. heryng vnprofetably erþly speche & fleschly siȝtes. For it is þe ryght dome of god þat ich man schal be /| medid after þat he trauell f. 127v for þe luf of god / Mannes. soul is cristes spouses and as a god wife is leuest to speke with hir husband byfor al. oþer men. & se hym & here hym. & loth to here or se. þat shold displ'ese hym:' So shold a cristen man. be leuest to speke with god in de'uout praier & holy redinges

Look at your own sins and at the joys of heaven.

3 Exterior ceci'ltas facit ut interius videatur *in margin.* 5 ow⟨t⟩ward: t *interlined with stroke.* 7 wold: r *interlined after* o.

& to here of his kyndnes & worthi'nes. in prechinges & (M. 98) in god comynyg /. low wat god seiþ to manes soul. canticorum 2 Surge propera amica. mea. sponsa mea. & veni ostende mihi faciem tuam. &c / Rise he seþ my luf / my spouses. hiȝe þe . & com to me. shew to me þi face. / þat is to mene shew to me þi face. þat is to mene. Rise vp̄ fro synne. man soul. þat shold be my luf by charite & my spoues. weded to me by trewe belefe. cum to me. my werkes of holy desire shewe me þi face. turne to me & not fro me let þi voise syng in myn eeris songes of gostely luf / lotħ shold a man be to here. or se any þing (M. 100) þat shold drawe hym fro þe luf of þis heuenly spouse iesu. Bot here now wat oure lorde seiþ to a soule þat can no delite fynd bot in erþly þinges & fleshly lustes. / Si ignoras te o pulcra inter mulieres. egredere &c. If þow knowest not þi selfe he seiþ þow feire among we'men.' Go owt & go away. after þe stepis of þi flokes. & fede þi geet cantici primo / An hidous blamyng seiþ seynt bernard it is and a sherp̄ þat god seiþ to sych a soul. go out & go awey Wen lordes or ladyes are wrotħ & gretly angrid.' þen þay sayn to her seruantys. or to her maydynes. Go fro me. go out of my sygħ go out of my house Such scherp̄ speche vsiþ crist þe spouse of manes soul qwen he seiþ þow feire amang wemen þat is þow soul. þat I mad faire among oþer soules wiche shold be my spwses. & my luf If þou knowest not þi selfe wos spouses þow art how þu art able. & þu wil þi self be blissed with me. & with myn aungell in heuen if þu haue no ioy to þinke on me to here & speke of me & of gostly maters.' Go out fro þe godys of þe soul. to fleshly desires fro inward rest of þi spirit to noyse. & trobyll of worldly bysines in qwich þinges is mycħ labur & sorow & torment of spiryt O how heuy is it to a cristen man wicħ is wont to haue meditacions of þe state of paradise. þat man was set in / of þe blisse & þe ioy þat man was ordeyned to wicħ is wont to þinke on þe godnes & þe gret maieste of god /.' & how he mygħt increse in vertu'ouse lifyng.'

Our Lord's rebuke to the soul of him who does not guard his senses.

8 belefe: *second* e *altered from* i. 22 sygħ *sic.*

For to go fro sich swetnes & ⟨to⟩ lustes & likynges of þe flesch / wich shold raþere be called desolacyons and harmes of þe fleshe þan likynges to go fro gostly rest to worldly. | rest to worldly troubyles & gruchyng of f. 128 conscience / þis chaungyng is to a gode cristened soul a maner of an hell / and to euery man & woman þat wilfully turnen to vnlefful lustes of lechery. pryd couetyse & sych oþer þe spouse crist seiþ go þow away after þe stepes. of þi flokis & fede þi geet / Þat is to mene þat such an euil. lifer is wers þen flokis of bestes wich feden here fles'chly appetite. with vnclene lustes & many fold faylshed which stynken. byfor. god fouler / þen geet to men. For a best hauyng no reson. if he do amys his kynd. excusiþ hym Bot reson acu'siþ a man which haþ reson & mysuseþ hit And for aman haþ fre choys. and fredome. & can deme wich is gode & w'ych is euyl. & doiþ ageyn þe dome. of reson þerfor. he shall be demed to hendles pyne. w⟨h⟩ere a best þat wantys. syche fre dome shal neuer so be demed And so þe peple þat shal be dampned endlesly shall be of wers condicion þen bestes wich dyen body & soul. and so þay shal go behynd bestes þat is to sey þay sall be wers þen bestes.' ȝhe wers þen stynkyng gete. to whom dampned folke are lykened mt 2 / loke we not þerfore. awey fro god. ny turne we not fro hym. Be we not euer totyng owtward as a bird (M. 102) doiþ in a cage. Be war man of þe catte. of hell þe lest he cach þe with þe clawes. of temptacion Loke oft inwarde in þi consciense how it standiþ þere speke of god. speke to god hym list to kys þe Osculetur me osculo oris sui let my spouse kys me with þe cusse of his mouþ seiþ þe trew spouses a gode cristen soul canticorum primo and þe seyng of þes wordys haþ þe spouses by inspiracion of þe spous / þis cusse. is a swetnes & a delite of hert so hony swete.' þat all worldly myrth in comparison þerof is bot byttemes. And oure lorde with his cusse.' kyses. no soul bot such. soules þat lufen noght

1 (2nd) to *interlined above expuncted* &. 18 w⟨h⟩ere: h *interlined with stroke.*

bot hym and for hym // lufe we þerfore. to speke of god and to here to speke of god byfor. all oþer spekynges and herynges / þus myc̄h is seid of þe witte of þe heryng / and spekyng þat longeþ þerto // Tastyng is þe þrid witt / which warly is to be keped For mych harme caches a manes. soul. by vndescrete etyng & drynkyng Seynt gregor. seiþ 30 moralium. þat a man fiȝteþ veynly ageyn oþere synnes bot if þe appetite of glotyny þat is within vs. self be first chastied / þe appetit of gloteny is within aman lyke to a treytour wyc̄h wold for. his owne lucre. betray þe cite in wic̄h he dwelleþ And veyn it were to any lorde. to fiȝt ageyn his enmyes. in þe felde wile rebel tratures dwellid vnchastised / in his cite qwerfor. in gostly batel. fi⟨r⟩st it is to fiȝt / ageyn gloteny for. but vnleful lust be foghten ageyn:' it will destroy all f. 128v vertues In figur qwerof /| it is red 4 regum 25 þat nabuȝardan. þat is to mene þe prince of cokis destr'oyed þe wallis of Ierusalem. Ierusalem is as mych to sey as siȝt of pees. and by þe walles. of ierusalem. ar vnderstonden vertuse For within vertu⟨o⟩s lifyng. dwelen al god men. þe prince of cokis is a manes. bely. to whic̄h cokis seruen. qwen it is so ⟨þen þe⟩ bely is gyfen. to gloteny of lusty metys. & drynkes it distroy⟨e⟩s vertuse. Seynt paule withstode þe prince of cokys. his bely wen he seiyd prima corinthiorum 9 Castigo corpus meum &c I chasty my body he seys. & bryng it into seruage. lest perauentur wen I preche to oþer I my self be made reproueable. / on fyue maneres. þe vọice of gloteny temptys a man / Prepropere laute / nimis ardenter studiose. Prepropere þat is to sone or to erly as many men son after þay are out of bed þay eten & drynken. without nede. bot for. lust <u>ecclesiastes 10</u> Seys Salamon <u>ve tibi terra &c</u> Who to þe erþe of wom þe kyng is a childe & qwos princes eten erly. þis erþe is aman for man was made of þe erþ

4 Gustus. *in margin.* 14 fi⟨r⟩st: r *interlined.* 20 vertu⟨o⟩s: o *interlined above* e *expuncted.* 22 þen þe *written over erasure; second word may have been* þt. 23 distroy⟨e⟩s: e *interlined with stroke.* 29 versus *in margin.*

& into erþe he shaƚƚ turne. þe kyng of þis erþe of man sholde be fre dome or wilfuƚƚ choise of amañ wat tyme þat a man demys. as. a childe. þat is to ete erly. & wilfully cheses to ete or drynke to erly and þe handes fete & mouþe wych are as prince vnder þis kyng executen. his foule lust ageyn reson wo to sicħ aman For as þe seruantes of god bygynen at morne to serue god after her connyng / so such glotons. of qwom her bely is her god as þe apostyl seis philippensium 3o quorum deus venter est &c Begyn'en first at morne. to þinke on hir wombe. ioy an hastily þey hyen hem qwat mete or drynke þay may come by:' þay snachen þeron as hogges. // þe secund temptacion of gloteny. is qwen men desiren to deyntey metys. or to costlew for to plese her tast qwer homly met ar sufficient. & holsom ynogħ / þe peple of Israel. led oute of egypte:' were not content with met sent to hem fro abufe. manna þat was. called aungeƚƚ met bot þe desired flescħ & god sent hem denteyouse. bryddes bot whiles þe flescħ was in her mouþes. þe wraþe of god feƚƚ on hem. and god smote gret multitude of hem̄ with detħt for her grochyng & her lusty mouþes numeri xjo // Þe þryd temptaciom of gloteny is nimis qwen a man is stired to to mycħ etyng and drynkyng To mycħ etyng was on cause of þe foule synne of Sodome eȝechielis. 16 / and Olofernes was slayn in his dronkennes. Iuditħ 13 þe fourt temptacion of gloteny is ardenter to ete to gredyly withoute dred or reuerence to god as Esau gredily etyng potage solde þe right of his primogeniture genesis 2 // // þe 5te temptacion of gloteny is St'udiose. a mañ to stody byfore. wat mete he may haue to fede /| his f. 129 lusty taste or elles how lusty his mete may be diȝte þus syned þe sunes of hely. prest primo regum 2. wich wolden haue þe flesħ os þe sacrifice þat was offered to god diȝt after here own lust ageyn þe lawe of god / Mete & drynke shold be reseyued. as nede askes to susteyn. oure kynd & not after þe stiryng of lust Bot discre'cion

12 Laute *in margin.* 22 nimis *in margin.* 26 Ardenter *in margin.* 29 Studiose *in margin.* 33 os *sic, for* of.

is to be had in þ^{is} mater For many a tyme. lust colorys hym self vnder nede so þat oft men wen þat hem nediþ to ete & to drynke. qwen it is no nede bot lust / Diuers remedies Doctors. wryten. ageyn þis temptacions of gloteny // þe first is gode. & besy occupacion Salomon seis prouerbiorum desideria &c desir|ringes slene þ^{e} slow man. his handes. wold wirke no þing al day he couetes. and desires / an ydel man is full of hunger / his eeres desire to here tiþinges. his eghen to se vanitese. his tast mete & drynke. Gode ocupacion lettes al. þes hungeres. & spe|cially þ^{e} first temptacion of to tymly etyng as experience proues // þ^{e} secund remedy is þat a man seke. in his etyng. sustentacion of his body & more desire holsom metys. be þey neuer so homly þen delicacyȝe & precius metys. For. as seynt austyn seys / mete shold be takyn as medcyn. let hunger. prouok þ^{i}n appetit / and no lustynes. and wen þ^{u} sittyst at a borde with oþer men loke not hyder & þeder qwat mete oþer men haue. byfor. hem / take hede. to god. and to þ^{i} selfe de= spise not þe mete. ny þ^{e} drynke þat standen. byfor. þ^{e} gruch not þof þow want sause. hungor and salte. ar sause god ynogh to an hole mañ for any mete as Seyn Bernard seys. þinke þat many aman better þen þow wo|ld hold hym payed of fewer metys. & viler þen þow art serued with and wald take for. deyntey þat þ^{u} settist lityl by / hold þ^{i} selfe vnworþ^{i} to fare so wel as þ^{u} doist þ^{is} maner of doyng and þinkyng is a gode help̄ ageyn þ^{e} secund temptacion of glo|teny þat mefis to lusty etyng / and drynkyng // þ^{e} þryd remedy is þat a man ete not to oft ny to mekyl wittyngly hard it is to gyf a mesure. qwat quantyte of mete & drynke is euen ynow. But þat a man besy hym by long experience. to kep̄ suc̄h a mene. þat he take not so litel þat his body may not susteyñ syc̄h labour as longes hym to do:' or elles þat he take so myc̄h þat after mete he may neþer wele pray. ne

10 primum remedium contra gulam *in margin*. B. 12 2^{m} *in margin*. B. 29 3^{m} *in margin*. B. 30 nota bene *in margin*. B. 31 an no mo *interlined, with caret, after* ynow.

rede or. do such besynes as longys to hym Euery manes own̄ experiense is best mays'tres in þ^{is} case / þis answeris to þ^{e} þrid temptacion. Ageyn þe fourt þat is to gredy etyng is þat a man swach not his mete as an hungry. hounde But ete tretably & ocupy his mynd wiles he etys with sum holy meditaciom of cristes passioun of heuen or hel or of þe houre of deth̄ or þinke on sum psalme or ympne or here sum holy redyng if þow be /| lettered / Ag^{e}yn þ^{e} fift temtacion of gloteny. is to stody f. 129^{v} byfore how lustily þou may be fed. is to þinke how son̄. lust passes and wen it is don̄. it is as it neuer had bene. & leues bihynd it remorse of conscience werfor. qwen þ^{u} felest such̄ lusty stirynges to gl'otonous fedyng / þinke as if þow had. such mete & þat þow were filled þerof and how wen it is passed. it is bot as a dreme // Thynke how lusty foode stires a man to ete þ^{e} more and mych̄ etyng & gredy etyng greues gọḍ þ^{e} stomake. Makys men seek And ageynword sobre etyng. kepis hele. It is liȝther / diffied It kepis fro mych synne homly liuelod nedys. bot litel. worldly besynes. ny no gret riches. and it is right̄ sauery to aman̄ þat is anhongired wen þe peple of israel. after long laboryng and werynes. in here iourneyng:' thrysed after water Moyses smote vpon̄ þ^{e} stone. & water flowed out qwerof þ^{e} peple dranke. exodi 17. & numeri 20 qwich water for it was to hem delicyose in her gret þryst:' 'it called hony in þ^{e} psauter psalmo 80 de petra melle. saturauit eos. secundum pari= siensem in de virtutibus. // Also sobrenes. of etyng & drynkyng ablys a man to many vertues. to chastite. to labour to war spekyng to lerne wele. It kepys. sadnes. of mynd. and gyfes god insoumpyl. to oþer It auayles to meryt of endles blyse For þ^{e} more þat we ab'steyn vs here fro lustes:' þ^{e} more haboundanse. haue we here of gostly godys. and þ^{e} more shal we receyue of end'les

3 4^{m} *in margin.* B. 9 5^{m} *in margin.* B.; fift: e *interlined after* t. 23 thrysed: t *interlined after* s, *with stroke.* 26 is *interlined after* it, *with stroke.* 27 þe *crossed through before* petra.

riches. / wysly þerfore. & warly is þ^{e} tast wic̄h is þ^{e} þryde. witt to be keped for. after it is gouerned. commys (M. 104) myc̄h profyt or. harme. to a manes soule // Smellyng is þ^{e} fourt wytt wysle also to be keped forbe. it fro any cristen creature to vse any swet smellyng thynges to stir oþer þerby to synne as sum wymmen vsynen swet anoyntmentes to stir men to lust as dottour de lira seis super 3^{m} capitulum ysaie In vengeanse qwerof þay suf- fered þerfor in seknesis an presonynges filȝt and stynke. Erit pro suaui odore. fetor ysaie 3° / Also noman be so squemus þat he lett for to visett & socour pore peple. & seke in here nede. We rede in þ^{e} lyfe of seynt hew. þat was bischop̄ of lincoln̄ þat his maner was. þat he wold / entir into þ^{e} howse of leperes by þ^{e} wyc̄h & wen he made. to departe þ^{e} men meseles. fro þ^{e} wymmen meseles.' al þ^{e} men meseles. were þey neuer so foule. ny styngyng he wold kys. hem. And qwat tym a worþi clerke wilȝam þat was chaunceler / of lincolne seyd vnto hym Seynt Martyn kyssyng meseles. heled hem. Bot ȝe hele not þ^{e} leperes. þat ȝe kyssen Seynt hew answerd / þ^{e} cusse of seynt Martyn clensed þ^{e} flesh of þ^{e} lepere But þ^{e} cusse of leperes heles my sowle. / No stynke ny. | f. 130 filȝte. withstode iesu oure Saueour bot þat he com- mened with seke men and heled. hem. / Ensoumpyl. þen takyng / of oure lorde. wonde we not for. no stinke. ny for no fylȝte to help̄ þ^{e} seke. and in her ned qwy shold not aman. þat sum tym delites hym to mych in swet smellynges.' suffer to heuy smell. specially in com- fortyng / of seke folke sum tym̄. remedy of his synne. (M. 106) siþen sekneses. ar helyd by medicynes contraryọṣe to hem as Phisicianse. seiyn Crist for oure synne suffered. in all his wyttys. in his siȝte he suffered. gret peyn qwen he siȝe his moderes. sorow. and of þ^{e} oþer maries of Ioh̄n þ^{e} Euangelist an his oþer frendys. how his discipules

The fourth sense is smell.

Christ in His Passion suffered in this sense, as in all others.

3 Olfactus *in margin*. 4 is *interlined after* also, *with caret* (?). B. 14 he passed *in margin*, *with stroke after* wyc̄h. 15 had *interlined after* he, *with caret*. B. 17 styngyng: k *written above* g *expuncted*.

flowen fro hym he weped with his owne eghen. his enemyes. blynd|felled hym. / he siȝe his enemyes make ioy and gladnes at his sorowe. / wen we se þen men make litel or noȝt of vs perchaunse. despise vs and lagh̄ at oure harmes wen we se oure frendys in dises.' þ^{is} pacience þat crist had. in his siȝt shold strengh̄ vs to be pacient / Clois|terers and ankers. and ankeresys. þat suffren wil- fully to be blyndefeld / þat is to sey þat her eghen be closed / fro siȝt of worldly vanite. and fro occacion of mych̄ synne. shold not mecle be staryng owtward. neþer gl|adly here vey⟨n⟩ tydynges neþer oþer vnprofetable talys wh|ech myȝt com liȝther to mynd in tym of prayng and let eghe of deuocion / Crist suffered in his heryng / (M. 108) reproueable. wordys. and scornfuli fals. lesinges ageyn his reuerence. and wordys of blasphemy and al he su|ffered as he had not herd hem Factus sum sicut homo non / audiens &c Psalmo 37 and þis he did for oure synne. / We þenne þat wilfully haue herd yuel. speche. and veyn speche ouȝt wele to suffre reproueable. wordys. fals. wordys. & schamfull̄ wordes spok|en ageyn. vs. in remission̄ of oure mysheryng Crist suffered in his tast / þ^{e} bitternes. of galle / Suffer we pacientli þenne þouȝe oure mete. or. drynke be not delicyuse to oure lust ny. gruche. we not with esi fare in maner byfore seyd For miche. and ofte haue we trespased. in etyng and drynkyng // Crist suffered in his smel. þ^{e} stynke of ded and roten careyns. in þ^{e} hill were he was crucified / Suffer we þerfor. in oure smell. in maner byfore. spokyn̄ / (M. 110) Crist suffered in in his towching / most herd pyne. scourged nayled and wounded In þ^{is} witte of felyng / he suffered ouerall in ich̄ party. of his body. For þe wytt of touchyng or felyng is in euery party of þe body and for. we synne with ich̄ a party | he vouched saue. of his mercy to suffer payn. for vs in ych party of his body. f. 130^{v}

We must expect to do the same.

The fifth sense is feeling.

The greatness of Christ's suffering.

1 visus *in margin*. B. 11 vey⟨n⟩: n *interlined, and later over-written by* B; audit[us] *in margin in faded ink*. 13 auditus *in margin*. B. 19 to suffre *in margin*. 22 gustus *in margin*. B. 29 in in *sic;* Tactus *in margin*. B. 33 of our body *added in margin after* party.

Also oueral. in his body he suffered dethes swote / For as seynt Bernard seiþ he weped not alone with his eghen bot with alle. his lymmes. / Quasi inquit membris omni-
(M. 112) bus. fleuisse. videtur þe angusch and þe peyn. þat he suffered in his flesc̄h for dred of his pynful passioun þat was toward was so gret:' þat he swate blode. qwen he preyd luce 22 And no wonder for þe. qwyker þat þe flesh̄ is and þe tenderer / :' þe hurt þerof is þe more greuouse as a litel. hurt in.þe eḡh greues more þen a grete stroke on þe bake. / Cristes. flesch. was most tendre taken of þe most clene maydeñ and ȝong / It was clenest fleshe. and best complexiond qwerfor. his peyn was greuestes A seke man is lete blode / not in þe membre þat is seke. bot in þe harme þat is hole. wiche bledeþ for al þe body / Was þer no hole man in al mankynde / qwerfor crist in quom̄ myȝt be no seknes of synne wich is called þe harme of þe fader Saluauit sibi dextera eius & brachium sanctum eius Psalmo 97. was let blod in his merciful. passioñ for þe saluacion of man kynde. / Siþen crist þen suffered þus passyng payne. in his touch-ing /. Wele aught ich cristen mañ and woman to kep̄ wele her handes and her oþer membrys fro vnclene touches. fro lechorouse kyssynges and foule dedys of þe fleshe. for. þorow filȝþ filthi touches. entres dedly synne / oft into þe hert / þow þen þat desiris to haue a clene hert:' kep̄ werly þi .v. wittes. byfor rehersed Sight. heryng. tastyng Smellyng and touchyng / qwich are as entrese of lijf or of deth̄ to þe soule and þen shalt þow wel fulfyll̄ þis precepte of Salomon. Omni custodia &c with all warde kep̄ þin hert for of it liif goiþ forþ. & þus endys þe first parte of þis tretys þe wiche shewes. how aman shold kep̄ his wittes outward

He was let blood for the sickness of mankind.

¶ If he will haue clennes. of hert þat is to sey of conscience // Bot forþermor. it is to witt þat þe wittes most warly be keped out'warde:' so most a man haue. an inward siȝt. þat is þoghtys and his intent be wele

33 2ᵃ pars *in margin against* ¶ If. B; *also in inner margin, in different hand, against* Bot.

A covetous man is like a fox.

He is like Saul and not like David.

gouerned inwerd // Oure saueyour seis Matthei .8. vulpes. (M. 128) foueas. habent & volucres celi nidos. Foxes he seys haue her holes. and brides. of heuen her nestis // By Foxes may. wele be vnderstonden. fals men / wịçħ men ⟨wily men⟩ þat setten al her hert in tresuryng of worldly gode For þey bigylen simple men as foxes. deseyuen briddes þat are simple as hennes. geese / & sucħ oþer and lyuen by falshed & rauyn as. foxes done. // An þat mor. is to sorow. sum cre-pen in to holis of þ[e] erþe as Saul entered in to a cafe 1° regum 24 for to do his filȝte þerin and to defoule þat stede // þus sum. | entren to (f. 131) pres⟨t⟩hod. sum to religion. sum to be ankers. and (M. 130) ankereses qwech maner of states. shold be not of comyn liifyng of þe worlde. Bot as contrary to þ[e] wold and hid fro þe world as folke þat dwellen in cafes. And ȝit many prestes. many monkys Chanons. Freres. ankyrs. and ankeresses Nunnys & heremytes are. more worldly. lifen more lustily. are more delauy in curiose talkyng of þe world an luken more after worldly reuerense & honour þen. þay shold haue. done dwellyng stil in þ[e] state of þ[e] world þat þay were first in or ellys in any worldly state þat euer þay shold haue commen to. In such priuate. astates. may þay do many preuey vnleueful. þinges more þen þay myȝt do if þey were in myddys þe world / Neþles ageynward many a man takys þe ordre. of prest / many taken þ[e] state. of religioñ or. of recluse. as Dauid entred in to þ[e] same cafe into wicħ saul entred / Saul as it is bifore seyd entrid in to þat hole. or. caf to de= foule. it But Dauid ẹnṭẹṛẹḍ ịṇ ṭọ þẹ ṣạṃẹ. fled þeder to defend hym selfe fro þe tyrauntry of Saul þat porsewed hym. þus sum enteren into degre or states before re= hersed for ease. and lust and þes defilen her astate. Bot þay þat taken þe ordre. of prest or entren in to religyon or. state. of recluse forto lijf in chastite / in penaunse

5 wily men *in inner and outer margins.* 12 pres⟨t⟩hod: t *interlined with stroke.* 13 nota per optime *in margin.* B; & *crossed through and expuncted after* comyn. *Letter erased after* comyn. 16 of Monkes, Nuns, &c *in margin.* L. 26 ny (*?*) *appears to be obliterated at the end of* many.

in preere. In holy redynges for to be. rom / of wor'ldy occasions. w⟨h⟩erby men & wemen fallen. into synne / þes entrene. with dauid & by her. gode entre & gode contynuance / in her degre þey scapen. her gostly enmyes.' as dauid scaped his bodyly aduersaries / þes deuout men & we'men are no Foxes. in condicions bot þay may be called brydes. of heuen.' for condicions þat þay haue like to þ^{e} proprietese. of briddes / On propriete of bryddes is þat þey forsakeñ þ^{e} erth & fly in þ^{e} eyre and fer fro þ^{e} erþe. most parte of briddes maken her nestes / þus gode peple. of what degre so þey be þey lufen erþly þinges bot for ned But þey desiren heuyn'ly þinges her bodyes laburen in erþe. bot þe ioy and þ^{e} rest of her soules.' is in hop̄ þat þay haue to com to heuynly blis þay vsen not wiles and frawdes. as foxes. But þey vs'en hem to kep̄ treuþ. charite pacience. compassion and oþer vertuse // A man þat shal make a cercle.' fixes þat on sid of his instrument / and stabyles it in a poynt and þat oþer sid of his instrument he ledys round aboute and so he makys a god compase But and þ^{e} parte of þ^{e} instrument þat was fixed.' be remeued.' he shal mak no god cercle þus shold a mañ in all his werkys. stabyl his

The good are like birds, for they fly up towards heaven.

f. 131^{v} intent //| in god þat his dedis were doñ to goddys worschip̄ and þenn shal his liif be so iust þat it shal. bryng hym to endles blis wiche is likened to a cercle þat has non ende. // But and his intent be set on any vntrewe. or ypocrise. or worldly. vanite.' þow spilles þ^{i} wirkyng. and þou3e þi dedis be gode.' þow leses þ^{i} mede // Make þerfor. þ^{e} nest of þin intent in heuen þorow trew desire and vnfeyned / to be goddes seruant // þe secund property þat of a brid is.' when he flies he holdes his hed lowe. / þusþ^{e} seruant of god / fli3e he neuer so hy by holynes. of lyfyng he. letys litel by hym selfe. and by his dedys. þus tau3t vs þ^{e} brid þat fli3e hiest crist iesus Cum omnia feceritis que precepta sunt vobis dicite serui inutiles.

2 w⟨h⟩erby: h *interlined.* 6 nota proprietates auium. 1^{a}: *in margin; a word following* nota *is crossed out and illegible.* B. 22 h. *crossed out after* in. 26 *letter erased before* on. 30 2^{a} proprietas auium *in margin*. B.

sumus luce 17 / When ȝe done al þinges þat are com⸗mounded to ȝow. seis crist / sey ȝe. of ȝour self we are vnprofitable seruantes Acordingly to holy scripture. þus writes a versifier / Si tibi copia seu sapientia forumque detur:' Sola superbia dest'ruit omnia si commitetur. / þis is þus mycħ to mene. / haue aman neuer so gret plentey of bodily riches. e⟨i⟩þer of gostly riches. as gode disposicions or. vertuse. or. ellys þat aman be wyse and witty or. stronge. and symle. If pride folow. any of þis. he destroyes. hem aƚƚ. here it is to aman þat haþe giftes bodily or. gostly. abouf oþer men to ber hym. mekely / But a man sho'ld consider as seynt gregory seis in an omely Sicut crescunt dona &c / þe mo gyftys. & þe gretter þat aman receyues. of god:' gretter rekynyng shal he make So þat þe more. þat a man rece'yues of god. þe more meke. & þe more ferd / ouȝt hym to be. leste for. pride & mysusyng of þe gyftes of god:' he be þe de'ppere dampned Qwerfor. as þe brid fleyng holdes his ⟨hed⟩ do'wnward / and low So euer þe wrþier þat þu art ay þe lower be þin hert ecclesiastici 3 Quanto magnus es:' humilia te in omnibus. / Lincoln' in a sermon þat bigynnes. Beati pauperes. Reherses. viij tokenes qwerby a. meke man may be knowen. / þe first is if he be vndermyned or repreued of his defoutes specyaly ⟨of⟩ on þat is lowere þen he. if he suffer it pacyently. with⸗owte indignacion Many man lakes. hym selfe & seis I know non so yuel. as I am my-selfe. But if anoþer mañ lake hym be it neuer so litel:' þenne wiƚƚ he be ful angry. // þe secund tokyn is:' if he be not wantoñ qwen he is in state of worchip̄ / Many qwen þey are pore and litel. set by semen meke & mylde. Bot wen þey com̃ to prosperite:' þay are wantoñ nyse of wordes and þinken þat þey may sey. or. do qwat hem list namly. amang porer and lowere ⟨men⟩ þen þey be // þe þryd signe of meknes. is:' If he

7 e⟨i⟩þer: i *interlined* 11 De humilitate *in margin.* 19 hed *written in margin with caret;* wrþier: *three letters* (?hit) *interlined after first* r. B. 21 Lincoln. serm. Beati pauperes *in margin.* L. 23 1m *in margin.* B. 24 of *interlined, with stroke.* 29 2m *in margin.* B. 34 3m *in margin.* B; men *interlined, with stroke.*

ȝeld not yuel for euyl. neþer cu⟨r⟩se for curse. bot raþer and ned be. he wil do gode ageyne yuel and pray for. f. 132 hem þat cursen hym / þe condicion of a prowde /| man. is þat he wold be syne abuf oþer men and þerfor. raþer þen mon sholde wene. þat his enmyes had þe better of hym ageyn alitel. yuel ded or a litel. yuel worde. done or seid ageyn hym. he wil do doubyll yuel. turne. or. speke a double yuel. worde. // þe fourt signe of meknes. is:' qwen a man emang his compers and his felowes. ise first redy. to do seruise redier to do seruise to his felowes. þen to take seruise of hem. / more wilfull amang men. of his degre to sit bynethe. þen to sit abuf // þe fifte is if he thanke lowly. and mekely al þat done. hym gode. or seyn hym gode þinkyng þat it is more of her. godnes þen. of his // þe sext tokyn is If aman. be als redy. to obey to his suffreynes. as he wil þat his sugettes obey to hym // þe Seuent is:' If he be aman. set in powere. he knowes raþer hym selfe. to be a suget þen a suffreyn̄ as Did Centurio wic̄h seiyd to oure lorde. Matthei 8 I am a man set vnder pouere and I haue knyg̅h̅tes vnder me. // First he knew hym selfe to be a soget. þẹṇ ạ ṣụffṛẹyṇ. to þe Emperour / and to his leue tenantes And þen after he seyd þat he hade sugettes vnder hym // þe 8 signe of meknes. is qwen a man is preysed / If he delite hym not þerin ny bere hym þe hyer / for his preysyng // Qwo þat haues þis 8 condicions:' he is a brid of heuen and ho⟨l⟩dys his hed ⟨lowe⟩. fliȝe he neuer so hiȝe / in vertue // þe þrid properte of a brid is þat qwen he fliȝes:' (M. 132) he spredis his wengys. brod & makys a crosse. of hym selfe þus þe seruantes of god / lif þey neuer so vertuusly. þey do penanse ȝhe for þe mor parte myc̄h more þen gret synners. do For comynly gretest synne⟨r⟩s don̄ lest penaunce. and litel. syne⟨r⟩s doiþ myc̄h penaunce /

1 cu⟨r⟩se: r *interlined, with dot.* 5 mon: *possibly* men. 8 4m *in margin.* B. 12 5m *in margin.* B. 15 6m *in margin.* B. 17 7m *in margin.* B. 23 8m *in margin.* B. 27 ho⟨l⟩dys: l *interlined, with stroke*; ⟨lowe⟩ *written in margin, with stroke.* 28 3a proprietas auium *in margin.* B. 32 synne⟨r⟩s: r *interlined, with caret.* 33 syne⟨r⟩s: r *interlined, with stroke.*

And many tyme as Seynt Ierom did þey sorowen more for. a venial. synne þen sum mañ dos þouȝe he had sleyn a mañ Briddes þat haue litel flesħ fliȝen wele so þat þey haue many federys as is þ^e pellicane. / þe ostrycħ & sych maner fowles þat haue mycħ flesħ. þay makę sembland as þey wald fliȝe. and beytn her wynges. boť her fete drawes euer vp̄ on þ^e erþe / þus many men makes countynance as þay wold do holy werkys & maken mycħ dyñ with her w|ynges. spekyng of holynes But her lifyng / is so fulł of fleshly lustes þat þey are no folowers of cristes passioñ But raþer scorners. of his passyon and so not partineris of his blis bot if þay amend hem & do verrey penanse Crist seys Luc' 15 þat þ^e aungelł of heuen ioyen on a synful man þat dose penaunce. for his synne <u>Penitentiam agente</u> He seys not þat aungelł make ioy for a man hetys to do penance / as slawe men do and gostly cowerdys // | Wech seyn we shall do f. 132^v penaunce. We shalł amend But þ^e begynen not / Neiþer he seis þat aungelł ioyen on hym. þat techen or prechen. Penaunce as many on prechen. or techen penaunce wicħ are cum|bered. with fleshly lustes and oft with synnes abhominable. neþer op|on hem þat semen. to do penaunce as ypocritys vsen. bot on hem þat don penaunce & crucifien. her flesħ withstond|yng fleshly vicese. &. punes⟨c⟩hyng her flesh for synnes by|fore done as þ^e apostle. writes galatarum. 5 // þ^e fourt propirte of a bird is:' þouȝ. þey sit and syng. on grene. bowes. ȝit most hem for ned of mete. and drinke liȝt downe. to þ^e ertħ But wiles / þey are vp̄on þ^e erþe. þey ben euer besy lokyng on ich side / ⟨for dred[e]⟩ of enmyes. & caching (M. 134) of harme. / þus þ^e seruantes of god þowȝ þey singe in here soules. songys of gostly gladnes when þey þinke. on þ^e blis of heuen wich neuer fadis bot is euer grene

6 betyn: y *crossed out after* b. 21 nota contra predicatores delicatos *in margin*. B. 22 *A word following* opon, *possibly* of, *has been obliterated*. 25. punes⟨c⟩hyng: c *interlined*. 26 4^a proprietas *in margin*. B. 30 for dred[e] *written in margin with stroke*, e *hidden by binding*.

þat is to sey fresc̄h & newe. / ȝit most hem com doune after þe comen nede of mane-kynde to ḥete. to drinke to speke to wyrke. to slep̄ Bot þen shold we. wele. ḷọẉ loke al abowte. þat we wer not cag̅h̅t in þe deuiles snare wic̄h as seynt Peter seis prima petri 5 / gose aboute as a roryng lyon̄ sekyng qwam he may deuoure. / Mic̄h temptacion is in etyng / In drynkyng / in spec̄h of worldly þinges / Qwer'for. gret circumspeccion nedys aman to haue in al. sic̄h dedis // þe fifte properte is:' hir nest is harde withoute & sherp̄ made of prikyng þornes and withine it is nesc̄h and soft þus þe seruantes of god sufferen sherpe penaunce in her fl'esh̄ scornes & many tribulacions // But withinforth in her consciences. þey haue softnes: of spirite gladnes of hop̄ & clennes. of hert / In nidulo meo moriar Iob 29. I wil dy in my litel nest / seis holy Iob as if he had seid as long as I lif to deth cum shal. I life sherply and suffer hard in my flesc̄h þat is withouteforþe þat I kepe clennes and softnes. of consciense withinforth and þis maner of lif'yng / may wel. be called alitel nest / after wic̄h sal̄l folow. gret rest in a gretter nest þat is yn þe blis of heuen / Bot sum maken her nest in þis warlde. contrariously soft without an hard and sherp̄ within For þey lifen in flesch'ly lustes & likynges and in her conscience within forth þey sufferen. gret prykyng and remorse. Sḥych peple sal. haue no rest bot mych sorow in þe gret nest of hel̄l qwer neþer þe body ny þe soule. shal haue any lust // þer is a preciouse ston̄ þat is called achates / wiche venymose / | f. 133 bestys dar not come nere. / A bird þat is called an erne puttys it in her nest for to kepe it fro venym. / By þis preciouse ston̄ is vnderstonden. oure lord iesus crist Be he myc̄h in þi mynde & in þi hert þinke qwat peyn he (M. 136) suffered in his flesc̄h withoute and how swet and softe he was. within in his hert And so shal þu dryfe awey. fro þi hert þe veyne. of inpacience. of gruch'yng of weriyng / & sic̄h oþer For rig̅h̅t it is and reson. þat þow. suffer peyn. for þin owne synnes. and for his luf þat

As the bird's nest is hard without and soft within, so must the servant of God discipline his flesh and keep his heart sweet.

As the eagle puts in his nest a precious stone, so keep Jesus Christ in your heart.

9 5ª proprietas *in margin*. B. 35 veyne *sic for* venyme.

suffered so mycħ sorow. for. þi synnes & for þe / haue þis stone. Iesu sadly in þi mynde. and þee þer not drede. þe veny'mouse serpent / of hel. // Dauid in þe psauter. (M. 142) likenes þe seruantes of god to iij briddes to a pellicane. to a nightrauen. and to a sparow. / a pellicane is an angry. and a wraþfull brid So wraþfull. þat oft tyme (M. 118) fo angyr he slees his owne briddys bot son̄ after he is full. sory. and makys mycħ mone. and þen he smytys hym selfe. with his bill. werwith byfore. he kylled his briddes and d⟨r⟩awes blod of his brest and with þe blode he qwykenes his bryddes þat wer sleyn. / þus shold a man þat with angyr and with wrath. slees his briddes qwech ben his gode dedys. / he shold be sorowfull. for. his synne and with his owne byl breke his brest /. þat is with sc⟨h⟩ryfte of his mouþe. þat he has synned with / drawe þe blod of synne oute of his hert and so shold he eft qwiken. ageyn his gode. dedis // Blod betokynes synne for diuerse causes. First. for as seynt austyn̄ seis / þe grounde of manes synne. is of þe corrupcion of blode of wich we are conceyued / Also a man þat is al. bebled is foule. and lothly to loke on in a manes eghe:' So a man defiled mych in synne. is foule in goddes eghe. / Also noman may wele iuge blode. to it be cold / So wiles þe lust of synne is hote:' þer is no riȝt dome in þe soule. Ensoumpul. wiles þe lust of lechery is hote. in a man Such a man þinkes þat lechery is to be don̄ and if any man stir hym to þe contrary he can not here. hym / aman þat is malyciously wroth is for þe tyme half wode / and as caton seis Ira impedit animam &c wraþe. lettys reson. of þe soule þat it may not se þe treuþe. But qwen þe temptacion is past:' þen a man seis his foly and wat harme commys of lechery wraþe an such oþer synnes. so þat after þe het of temptacion sewes þe right dome

See that you be not wrathful like the pelican.

3 Assimilacio dauid seruorum dei ad tres aues *in margin*. B. 7 fo *sic*. 10 d⟨r⟩awes: r *interlined, with stroke*. 15 sc⟨h⟩ryfte: h *interlined, with stroke*. 20 Cur peccatum comparatur sanguini *in margin*. 32 commys: *the last stroke of the second* m *is interlined and stroked for an* i. 33 Remedia contra iram *in margin*.

of synne Many remedyes we fynde for to kele þe hete. f. 133v of wrath of wich synne we speke nowe in aspecyal. If a (M. 122) man missay þe or mysdo. þe:ʼ þinke | anon þat þow art erþe. And þinke how it is bot right to trede opon þe erth and þinke if þow barke ageyn þine euyn cristen or. þin enmy. with malicyouse wordes to venge þi selfe þow. art of þe houndes kynde. and if þow stinkest ageyn doing a wers ded for a wiked ded. þu art a nedderes kyndel and not cristes seruant / of qwom þe prophet seis ysaie 53 Sicut ouis &c þat is to mene. þat after þe shamful. pynes. þat he. had suffered on þe nyȝt in wich he was takyn and on þe morne sueyng þey led hym to þe deȝte an dryuen. nayles ful. kene. þorow his handys and his feet and henged hym. as. a thefe. and in al. þis peyn. he made no more noise ny crie nye dose a shep qwen he is led to be sleyn. eiþer a lambe qwen he is cleped / Thynke also þat word is bot a⟨s⟩ wynde to feble. is a thyng. and bot as a poudre and dust þat a litel puftọf wynde. may ouercum. Wold þow þanke god in all aduersitees. and put hem. vnder þi fete. as settyng noȝt by hem þey shold ⟨help⟩ to lifte. þe vp to heuen./ Seynt andrew myght wele. þole. þat an hard cros. lift hym vp to heuenward / And þerfor. he desired hit / Seynt steveyn sent laulence. Seynt kateryne. seynt luce (M. 124) and al marteris ioyfully suffer'eden tribulacion and we wreches can not paciently suffer on. vnkynworde. / litel fire is sone blowen owte. with a litel. wynde. But gret fire is incresed by gret wynde So qwat man has. bot litel. luf to god and to his euen cristen:ʼ A. litel. worde will sone qwench it / But neiþer deth ny any oþer tribula- cion as seynt poul. wyttneses. romanorum .8. may depart a man fro god. þat is strong / in charite / A man þat ley in presone and shold be hanged or hedid bot if he peyed a gret ro'wnson. / wold he cun a man gret thanke. þat

Against wrath, think of the patience of Christ and the saints.

The windy puff of a word.

Remember what God has forgiven you.

7 prickist or *inserted in margin after* þow (2), *with caret*. B. 9 kyndel: ig *added in different ink and hand.* 17 a⟨s⟩: s *interlined, with stroke.* 21 shold: d *in different hand over erasure;* help *interlined, with stroke.* 24 laulence: r *interlined after second* l, *with caret.* 28 s *crossed out before* has.

wold cast a bage. with als mych gold as. wold raunson̄ hym ageyn his brest / Such a presonere wold be so glad. of þe money þat shold delyuer hym þat he wold no⟨t⟩ be wroth̄ with þe man þat cast þat golde ageyns his⟨e⟩ brest þoȝe it hurted hym But raþer he wold. luf hym / (M. 126) All men and wemen are presoners in þis world. / and we owen gret dett þat is to sey we ow'en to do. and suffer gret penance. for oure synnes & þerfore we seyn dimitte nobis debita nostra sicut & nos. dimittimus debitoribus nostris Matthei 6. Fader in heuenes. we seyn. forgif vs oure dettes. as we forgyfen oure dettours. / all myswordes þat men seyn. to vs. or of vs. and al wronges þat men done to vs if we suffer hem paciently. in oure soules. ȝhe þoȝe þe / | f. 134 flesh gruch þerwith ȝit þey ben a. parte of oure rownson̄ and quytyng of oure det / For as doctoures seyn / Aduersitees qweþer þey com. of þe visitacion of god as seknes. and losse of catel. eiþer of þe malice of man as wronge defamyng / or woundyng Eiþer of þe deuyl as hidouse. temptacions of wanhop̄ or. mysbylefe so a man consent not to such̄ temptacions all such̄ tri= bulacions if þey be pacien'ntly suffered. þay are payng of det for. oure synne as is penance þat a preste enioynes. for. synne. & þerfore. as towching harmes þat men do to þe.⸗ Thinke qwat crist seis luce 6. Dimittite & dimittetur vobis Forgyf ȝe and it shall be forgyfen to ȝow. as if god seid þus to þe þow art endeted to me. þow owest to me agret summe.⸗ If þow will ⟨þat⟩ I forgif þee.⸗ Forgif þow al. yuel. will. and rancor of hert / to hym þat has trespased. to þe / And þouȝ þe þinke it pe'ynfull. to þe to do þus.⸗ þinke on þe presoner bifore seyd. how gl'ade. he wold. be of his rounson̄ cast ageyn his brest þouȝ it hurted hym. And þinke þat þow art a gostely presonere and gretly endeted ageyn god and owþer most þi raunson be payed here þat is to sey trew. & dew

3 no⟨t⟩: t *interlined, with stroke.* 4–5 his⟨e⟩ brest: e *inserted between words.* 15 Aduersitas pacienter lata est pars satisfaccionis *in margin, perhaps by scribe.* 26 þus to þe *crossed out and* if men be in dedted to þe *substituted in margin, with caret.* B. 27 þat *inserted by crowding.*

penaunce for. þi synne or. elles. þow shal. be hanged or brente in hel or in purgatory. And so þin emnye If þow be paciently. dose þee raþer god þen harm̄ For he is a laundere (M. 124) þat helpes. to wasch away þi synne andalso he helpis to make þe a crowne in þe blis of heuen / We red in vitis patrum þat an holy man kyssed and blissed þe hand of a man þat had smyten hym Forqwy. he seyd þat hand had be'lded ⟨to⟩ hym. þe blis of heuen. / Seynt poul. seis romanorum. 8. þat al þinges turnen hem to gode. þat lufen god and þerfore male fessoures. & bakbiters. chiders cursers and such oþer harmen hem: self But þey profyten to godmen qwom þey disesen. For þey are occasion of increce of here mede. If here. were a man had xx pounde. of wich̄ money he gyfes in almes. to poore men xli. If þeues came and robed hym of þe oþer x pounde.ʼ or. men with fals chalenge made hym to lese. x li or. fals dettures. bare hym awey ·x pounde. or. ellys by any oþer chaunce. þat he lest x pounde.ʼ If he couþe suffer pa'cyently. þe losse of þe ten pound he shold haue mede for þe x pounde. as. for þe x pounde þa he dalte. in almes. // To gyf pore men money is a dede of almes. and to þanke god qwen þow has losse. and lowly to suffer it.ʼ is a ded of pa'cyens. and pacyence by all doctoures. is a⟨l⟩s god as doyng of almes / holy Iob is more com-mended in scripture for his pacience in aduersite.ʼ þen for. his almes. þat he did in prosper'ite / And þerfor. lese not charite by vnskylful wrath̄ for noȝt þat men can sey or do þe And if þow stumble and synne in wraþe /| f. 134v in any hastines qwiken ageyn þi god dedes. With sorow of hert and schryfte of mouþe. taking ensoumple. of þe pellican in maner byfore. seyd. // An oþer propirte has þe pellicane. as clerkes seyn he is euer leene. and þerfor (M. 132) he may fleȝe þe better / þus þe seruant of god. shold hold his flesh̄ so lowe. þat it drow. hym no downe. notably

2 Quibus comparatur inimicus *in margin*; emnye *sic*. 8 to *inserted in margin with caret*. 15 Paciencia equiparatur elemosine *in margin*. 18 chaunce: *long* s *inserted between* u *and* n *in different hand*. 24 a⟨l⟩s: l *interlined with stroke*. 31 pelicanus semper est macer *in margin*. B. 34 no *sic*.

wen he sholde. be gostly ocupied / þe scripture seis deuteronomii 32. Incrassatus est dilectus. & recalcitrauit (M. 136) þat is to mene many a creature. þat are lufed of god / and shold luf hym ageyn enterly qwen þey haue fatnes. or worldly riches. and licorouse metes & drinkys þey keken and wynsen ageyn god / and his lawe / and leten her flesh haue his will. and maystre ouer þe sowle / qwich shold be soget to þe soule. A wonderfull knot and a (M. 138) wonderfull mariage. is betwene þe soule. wiche is on þe hiest þing / vnder god as seis ⟨seynt⟩ austyn. and þe flesh wich is so vile a thing / Neþeles as doctoures seyn þis knot and þis betwix manes soule. and his body is gode. and profit'able for many skylles. First for. þerby is shewed þe gretnes of godes myȝte þat may ioyne to geder in þe makyng of a person. þinges þinges þat are so fare asonder. in kynde for þe soule. is a substanse vnbodily. and þe flesh is a subst'anse bodily. and ȝit þes ij ioyned togeder. maken a man Also þerby is shewed. þe gret godnes of god. qwich wil þat bodily creatures. be partiners. of his blis and þat myght not be bot if a body. were ioyned to a spirituel creature. for part hauyng of goddes blis:' is by vnderstandyng and knowyng of god. and also lufyng of god. wich vnderstandyng and luf. are in þe soule. But after þe general resurreccion qwen al menes soules. & wymmenes shal be knyt ageyn to her bodyes. þen of þe blisfull knowyng / & luf of god þat shal be. perfourmed þe perfeccion of al maner of bodyes. in þe soules of saued people. shal. redounde gret blis into her bodies in wych blis shal be performed. þe perfeccion of al maner bodies For al bodies heuenly. as sune. mone & sterne. and erþely as bestes stones & treese. are ordened to serue man genesis primo & deuteronomii 4° þat man ta'kyng seruice of hem shold ⟨so⟩ serue god þat he shold come to full blis of soul and of body / Gret profit comes. also both to body and soule. by þis knyt

The marvellous connexion between flesh and spirit.

10 seynt *interlined with stroke.* 12 mariage þat is *written in margin, with caret after* þis (2). B. 27 al: *dot stands between* a *and* l. 33 so *interlined with caret.*

tyng For wen a man for gyftes or any gostly godys. is stired to pride or. veynglory. consideracion of þ^e vilnes / and filȝt of his flesch̄ plukes hym doune to meknes. & wen a man is stired to gloteny. and lechery and such̄ lustys of his flesch̄.ʼ þ^e worþines of þ^e spirite seyng wat harme shold come þerby both to þe body and soul. f. 135 þinkyng also wat / | Ẉḥạṭ Senec seys. þat a man is made to haue gretter worship̄ þen to be. a seruant / to his flesh̄.ʼ oft tymes withstoundes such temptacions & so eiþer forþeris oþer For. þouȝ. þ^e body be in sum þinges. contrary to þe soule.ʼ In sum þinges it is helpyng to þ^e soul in maner bifor seyd. / And also wiles þe body and þ^e soul. are knyt to'gedir a man haue he. don̄ neuer so mych synne. he may do frutful penance. for his trespase wich penaunce may not be don̄ by þ^e body. and þ^e soul ons. be departed. discretly þerfor is þ^e body. to be gouerned of þ^e soul neiþer to streyt ne to large. For as. Ierom seis Non mediocriter he erris not a litel. þat preferis þ^e lesse gode. byfor þe more gode as þey þat maken more of abstinence þen of charite. as sum fasten so mych̄ to þey fall in a frenesy. or. sum oþer seknes. þat þay may neuer serue god with her body. as þey myȝte byfore. / And on þat oþer syde Fede no man his flesh̄ so fatte neþer kep̄ it so ranke þat it be to sloggy. and to slepy. dulle. to godnes. redy to lechery. // But kep̄ it in such a mene. þat it let not þ^e soul to sty vp̄ by heuynly meditacions and þat it be helper to þ^e soul. in go'stly occupacions as þ^e flesh of þ^e pellican̄ helpys and lettes not hym. to fliȝe vp̄ bodyly. þat a man̄ may sauely say Similis factus sum pellicano Psalmo 105 þat is I am (M. 142) like. to apellican̄ þe secund maner of brid werto dauid likenes þ^e seruant of god is a nyghtrauen. whos. kynd is to flegh on nyȝtes & biget his mete. / wilde bestes as þe sauter seis Psalmus 103 In ipsa pertransibunt omnes bestie &c on nightes gon̄ on raueyn os foxes. an wlfes. þus mysgouerned peple. on niȝtes don̄ mykyl harme. as

Comparison with the night-raven.

25 an to *interlined after* slepy. B. 30 Psalmo *in margin*; 105 *sic, for* 101. 32 Nicticorax *in margin*. B.

the'fes. þen robben. and kyllen. Glotons. vsen þen. here ryot lechoures. þen haunten. her filth̄. Bot þe seruantes of god fleghen þen with þe nigh̄trauen. by heuenly meditacions & by deuoute orisones. seken after grace. and men gyfen to stody are þen. besy. to fede. here soules. with hossum redyng But most longis preyng on nightes to peple of priuate religiones as munkes. chanones. Nunes. ankers. & hankeresses For þe psalme seis þus. / Factus sum sicut nicticorax in domicilio / þat is to sey I am made. as a niȝtrauen in þe euesynges of a howse þes peple of religioñ dwellen in houses ioyned to þe chirch̄ and foule it were bot if þey þat are ioyned. by bodily d'wellyng to goddes house were more ioyned to. god by heuynly deuocion þen oþer peple. and ofter vsed preyers boþe niȝt. an day. and þerfor. suyngly seis þe prophet vigil'aui / þat is I was waker / for. to contemplatife. peple as men / | & wemen of religioñ sholde be. wich̄ f. 135v haue her lyuyng by hir labour of actiue peple. It falles to wake. and prey for. such actiue peple. It is wretyn (M. 144) ecclesiastici 31 vigilia honestatis tabefaciet carnes / þat is. to mene as lire seis honest wakyng in preier and redyng of holy scripture shal refreyne. þe flesh fro fleshly lustis / lo wat crist seis to al men matthei 26. vigilate. & orate &c Wake ȝe he seis and prey ȝe. þat ȝe enter not in to temptacion an luce 12. crist seis Beati serui &c Blyssed be þe seruantes. whome þe lorde shall̄ fynd wakyng when he comes & iesus hym selfe as þe gospel. recordys luce 6 waked all̄ nyȝt in preiyere and so he tauȝt vs to wake. Not only with his word. bot also with his dede // viij þingys shold stir vs. to wake. in godnes.' þe first is þe shortnes. of our liife // þe secund is multitud of oure synes. // þe þrid is. þe wey þat we walken. in þat is þe worlde is full of pereles // þe fourt ow gode

Eight reasons for watchfulness.

2 l *crossed out before* ryot. 6 hossum: *top of first* s *is shaped like* l. 11 chirch: as euesynges of þe chirch *added in margin*. 25 an: d *interlined with stroke after* n. 28 viijto monerent nos ad uigilandum in virtutibus *in margin*. B (rent *above line with caret*). 33 ow: ur *interlined in darker ink after* w, *probably by* B.

dedys are fewe. and feble. / þ^e fifte is deth þat we are. sekyr / of Bot we wot not w⟨h⟩en. ny where ny how we shal. dye. // þė sext is drede of þ^e streyt & iust rekynyng þat we shale ȝelde at þ^e dome. // þe Seyuent is þ^e drede of þ^e hydouse peyn. of hell þat wilked peple shal suffer endlesly. // þe eght / is þe gret mede. in þ^e blis of heuen þat we shall haue. if we do wele / wicħ we sal. lese if we do yuel. // who so has wele þes. eght þinges in his ⟨m⟩ynd It will. shake a wey þ^e slep̄ of yuel sleuþe. many a tyme on nyghtes when a man neiþer sees nor. heris þinges þat myȝte lett hym of his bedys. of holy meditacion or of ḥọly ⟨honest⟩ / stody / þen is oft þ^e mynde & þ^e witte more clere & most swete. to god and nothing beris (M. 146) wittnes of þ^e gode þat a man dose. þen bo⟨t⟩ his god aungel. þat eges hym to gode. / þe boke of hester makys mencion in many pla'ces how þ^e preyer / of quene hester plesed mycħ þ^e kyng Assuer / hester in ebrewe is as mycħ to sey in inglysħ as. hid / And assuer is als mycħ to sey. as blesednes þat þ^e praier of hester pleised þen assuer /: It betokynes þat preiers þat are hid fro manes. knowyng as preyers done on nyg̅h̅tes ar mych plesing to god þat is most blessed ij maner of gode dedes þer are. / on maner is of such dedes as men are bounden to / by þ^e comyn lawe. as prestes to sey her matynes. messe and euensong. and þ^e peple is bo'unden certeyn houres on holy daes. to here diuyne seruise Men are bounden to fast ymber dayes & vigles of certeyn festes Euer þ^e opener þat such dedis are done þ^e better it is for. ensoumpul. of oþer f. 136 Bot oþer dedis of / | deuocion or. priuat vowes þ^e priueer þey are done: þ^e more war and wise is þ^e wirker / and to bost of suche dedis is ful perelouse: lo what þ^e sauter seis <u>vt quid auertis manum tuam & dexteram tuam de medio sinu tuo. in finem. Psalmo 73.</u> þat is why drawest þow owte þin hand and ȝyt þi rig̅h̅t hand fro myddes

Good works should be done in secret.

2 w⟨h⟩en: h *inserted above.* 5 wilked *sic.* 8 ⟨m⟩ynd: *first minim omitted and added later in paler ink.* 12 honest *in margin marked for insertion after* ḥọly. 14 bo⟨t⟩: t *interlined with stroke.* 21 bona facta dicuntur dupliciter *in margin.* B.

þi bosom to an hende / þi right hand is þ^{i} god. warke. / þ^{i} bosom betok'enes. priuete. Why þen drawes þow oute þi right hand þat was done in priuete. by bostyng or. desiryng þat it sh'old be opin knowen. for. þi veyn ioy and worldly vanite. and so þ^{i} mede is sone at an hende. wic̄h elles shold be hen'dles. // Seynt gregory seis it is (M. 148) mych madnes. to do gret þinges wherby a man may deserue heuen:' and lese it for. a wy'ndes pufe. or a manes preysyng / þ^{e} scripture tellys exodi 4 þat when moyses. drow his hand out of his bosum it ap'ered. leprouse. in tokyn þat gode dede done priuely qwen it is afterward made opyn by bost. an veynglory. it is lothly in goddes si3te as meselry is in manes sig̅h̅t of hem þat spillen her

A fig-tree dies if men strip its bark;

gode dedys. in sich maner pleynes god hym selfe. Ioel primo and seys þus. <u>Ficum meam decorticauit nudans spoliauit eam. & proiecit / albi facti sunt rami eius</u> / þe boster or þ^{e} veynglorier / of his gode dedys. has had awey þ^{e} berke of my. fige tre. he has. spoiled. it and made. it naked / and cast it awey and þe. braunches þerof are. made. w⟨h⟩yte / þe fige tre þat beris swet (M. 150) frute. betokyns a man þat dose gode dedys. þe. berke or þe rynde. þat kepes þ^{e} tre in qwyknes and fro harm̅ bitokynes. þ^{e} hidyng of such gode dedis fro desire of manes preisyng / þe rynd or. þe berke. of þ^{e} fige tre is gren̄ and as gren ouer all colours. nurishes. most þe

so does a good deed perish if it is proclaimed.

sight:' so when a man in his desire hides. his gode dedis fro veyn preysinges bifor. goddes si3te / When it is so þen þat a man dose gode dedes. as is prechyng or. bedys bedyng or. doyng of almes. for to purches. þerby. any worldly auansment or. furþerying of famouse presyng:' þen he makes. naked. þ^{e} figetre and spoiles hym of his gren barke. and so þ^{e} braunches are able to fire and not to brynge forþe. swete. frute.:' for. such a man by his pride and his coue'tyse. priuese hym selue of grace. þat þe endles frute þat shold haue commen. of his gode dedes

12 opyn by *written as one word with separation indicated*; an: d *interlined with stroke after* n. 18 *One or two letters erased after* spoiled. 20 w⟨h⟩yte: h *interlined with stroke.*

is dried / vp̄ and he. and al̄l his lymmes. arren disposed to be brondes of hell. fire. But if he do trewe penance for. his fals and feyned intencion // Seynt gregori seis / Depredari desiderat qui thesaurum publice in via por-tat þat is to sey he þat beris opynly tresure. in þe wey þat is full. of þeefes. and roberes.' he desires to be robid of þat tresure þis world. is bot a wey oþer to heuen or to hel and it is full of micheres of hell. as wiked spirites f. 136v þat stiren vs to pride // | Iịt is full. of men and wymmen flaterers. & gloseres. þat mayntenen men. in her pride and in her bost / what tym þen þat men seyn opynly. her gode. dedis as sum seyn. I haue fasted I thanke god. ich friday þis vij ȝere. bred. &. water I. lay in no shetys þis iiij ȝere. Seis an oþer I gyf ilke weke. xij d in almos / (M. 152) Seis þe þrid men þat spekyn þus forto be preysed. of men wat is it bot if þey seyd. I bere tresur opynly. and þus þey are spolied. of endles. med. for. þey receyuen. her. her mede. as crist seis Matthei 6 receperunt mercedem suam. It is not wretyn for noght þat iij kynges. þat comen to offer / to crist in his childhode couered her offerynges to þey com to his presence and þen þey opened hem. Matthei 2 apertis thesauris suis &c In tokyn þat vertuose men. shold. desire hire gode dedes to be keped preuey. til þey cam byfor þe maieste. of god were alle hertes shal be knowen opynly. / Folow we þen þe niȝt rauen. wich flies aboute. his purches. in nyghtes þat our dedys of deuocion be done priuely. in as mych as in vs is But if it be in any spe'cial. tyme. þat it is spedefull. to make hem knowen for gifyng of god ensoumple. or. sum oþer gostly cause / all þat is Done in priuete wat tyme so it is done.' it is done as in nyght // þe þrid maner of brid wherto dauid. likenes þe seruant of god. is a sparow. / A. sparow as clerkes seyn. þat sp⟨e⟩ken of proprietees. ọf brynges. furþe. many egges. and of hir eggys many briddes and nurishes hem bisily she makes hir nest in hay. and federes. she castes filȝte out of hir nest and kepis it clene / þus goddes seruantes haue many

He who carries a treasure conceals it.

Do good in private, as the night-raven flies by night

31 Passer *in margin.* 33 sp⟨e⟩ken: e *interlined with caret.*

god þouȝtes of endles þenges. and heuenli purposes. qwich are betokend by egges. for her roundnes. / and of her gode purposes. þey bryngen forþe gode. dedis which stien vpward as briddes. done. and her god. dedis þey nuryshen by perseuerance þay maken her nestes in hay and federys. For when þey a stir|ed to any presumpcion. of her gode werkes:' þey þinke how frely þey ben. and fadyng as is hay. and howe with a litel hete of pride:' her gode dedys may sone dwyne and Dwelke to noght / And. qwen þey are stired to despeir or. wanhop̄:' þen þey fliȝen vp̄ as federes. and þinken on. her gode dedis and on goddes godnes. / And þus þey fynden ease:' as sperowes done. in her nestys when such temptacions comen / Filȝte of synne þey casten owte. of her hertes by þe sacrament of penaunce and kepen hem clen by fleyng of occasiones of synnes. Anoþer propirte of a sparowis þat he flees þe habitacion of wild bestys. as wodis & lufes /| to duell ner men. / þus þey þat will plese f. 137 god:' mest fle. þe company of bestily. men. and drawe þam to resonable lifers For wiked. feliship̄ is on of most occasiones. of synne / Petre þe apos|tyl. wiles he was with crist and his disciples. was fer|uent / to suffer. for crist /. Bot when he cam in wiked felichip̄:' þe ministeres of þe yuel. Bischop̄:' Forsoke his lorde. Toby fled þe company of ydolatrys. and drowe to hym men þat dreden god. tobie Primo & 2° / Morouer a man shold not allonly. fle euyl company. But it is holsum and profetable. to a

Be solitary as the sparrow on the house-top.

man oft tyme to fle al. maner company and be solitary by hym selfe for þe psauter seis þus Factus sum sicut passer solitarius in tecto. þat is to sey I am made as a. sparowe. þat is alon vndur þe roffe. / how gode it is (M. 154) to be alone boþe þe olde law and þe newe. maken mynde

Examples of solitude: Isaac.

genesis 24. We rede þat þe patriarke. ysaac. ȝode oute. to haue his medita|cions in þe feld ageyn euyn. And

3 qwich are *crossed through after* purposes. 6 a *sic.* 9 dwyne, Dwelke *expuncted and* waste, cum *written in margin*. B. 16 and oþer prosperitese *crossed through after* synnes. 33 Vtilitas abstrahendi a tumultu populi *in margin*. B.

þer he mett with Rebecca. þat is to mene with goddis grace. Rebecca interpretatur multum accepit / Et quicquid habes meriti preuentrix gratia donat / Nil. deus in nobis preter sua dona coronat // Also genesis 32. Iacob abod by his one. fro all. his meynȝe. for to prey þe more deuoutely. and þere an aungel apered to hym. and blissed hym and told hym. þat he shold be called Israel. þat is to sey a man seing god // The holy wedowe Iudith. made to hir a closet In þe wich she dwelled with a few. of hir maydenes preuey fro þe peple. qwere she fasted. & (M. 158) wered þe hayre and prayed Iudiþ. 8. // Seynt Ioħn þe Baptist of whom oure lord seyd þat among wifes sones rose neuer non better whicħ was borne þorow miracle of a bareyn woman. wich also was halowed in his moderis wombe.' he dred so mecle þe com'pany. of men. specialy for spekyng / þat he fled into wildernes / lest he sholde be defiled. with speche / þus synges þe chircħ in his ympne. Antra deserti &c ne leui saltem &c lo wat ysai seis ysaie 7. ve mihi quia vr pollutus labijs. ego sum. wo to me he seis for I am filed in my lipes. and he telles skill qwy In medio populi polluta labia habentis ego habito þat is I duel. amog pepil. þat haue filed lipes. lo how goddes prophet seis þat he was filed þorow þe (M. 160) wonyng among men / Be it neuer so bright metal. gold. siluer Iren or stele. bot it shal. drow rust to it if it lige. long by metal. þat is rusted / For þi Seynt Ioħn Baptist fled þe feliship̄ of men And forto shew þat it is harde. to fle euyl. men. bot a man fle also gode men.' he fled (f. 137v) þe feliship̄ of holy men. of his own̄ / | kyne þat were of cristes kyn. as. touching his manhod and woned in wildernes. / And what begate he þere.' he begate þere þat he was. goddis babtist / þere þe. blissed. trinite was. shewed to. hym. þe fader in þe. voise þat was. herd fro heuen. þe son in his manhod. and þe holi gost in liknes of a doufe. / he. begate þere iij þinges. priuelege of prechour / meryt of marter-dome. and mede. of maydenhod. And þes. iij prechoures marteres and maydenes. haue special

St. John the Baptist.

2 Versus *in margin*. 19 vr *sic*. 22 amog *sic*.

crownes in heuen þat are called aureals. by sid her essencial med. and þes iij gat sent Iohn̄ by solitari liife. / Gabriel. messenger of our saluacion. fonde. oure lady solitari in gret de|uocion Ingressus ad eam luce primo / We fynd not in holy writ þat aungeles oft apered to men. in throng / Crist hym self after his baptym went to be by his on. in wildernes. and þer he fasted xl. dayes. Matthei 4. &. marci primo. to shew þerby þat among prese. of peple it is hard. to do trew penance. doctor de lira super marcum capitulo primo markes. how þat crist wich came. to preche þe treuþe. bifor þat he preched. did þis ij þinges fasted and went in to solitari place. (M. 162) enfourmyng prechoures. and techers of goddes law þat þey shold. first do penance. and chastise þeyre flesh̄ or þey taght̄ oþer men to do penance and cha|stice her flesh̄ / þus. did sent poul seyng prima corinthiorum Castigo corpus meum. &c þat is to sey I chastise my body. and bring it into seruage. lest I þat prech oþer be founden repreueable my selfe. / Crist infourmes also prechou⟨r⟩s in þat he ȝede to solitari place. þat soli-tarines. is profetable to contemplacion wher a man may. geder by prayere study and meditacion what he shal sey to þe peple in sermonyng / Crist in wildernes. suff|ered. þe fend to temp̄ hym. and þer he ouercam hym in tokyn þat deuil. is ful. besy to tempt solitari peple. And ȝit so|litari folk mych ouercomen hym. Crist whome no noise mi|ght let of preying / ny distrobul hym in his bedis he ȝed fro his discipules. into an hil. to be. by him

The hermits. self on þe nigh. when. he shold preiy luce 6 Paul and antony hillari and. Benet / & many oþer men. & wemen fleden compeny for to haue. homlines with god. and deuocion / Seynt Ierom seis Quociens inter homines fui minus. homo recessi / þat is as oft tymes. as. I. was among men. I. went a. wey lesse man̄ þen I came. It was asked. of a philosophur what þing was most noyus.

16 sent: y *interlined after* e *with stroke.* 20 Nota quomodo quis adquiret materiam predicandi *in margin.* B; prechou⟨r⟩s: r *interlined.* 25 þe *in margin marked for insertion after* þat. B.

to a man An he answerd þat amang al. creatures. no þing was so noyuse to a man. as an man. is to an oþer For when a man comes amang oþer men yt is full. hard f. 138 But if oþer he hurte þeym in worde. ded / . | or. en⸗soumpul or. þey hym For þ^{i} seis þ^{e} wise mañ ecclesiastici 18. Ne ob'lecteris in turbis nec in modicis. Est enim assidua commissio illorum þe meynyng is as lira seis Delite þe neiþer in mych meynȝe. neiþer in litel meynȝe. for þey sinen oft / And if þ^{u} be a gode man þat art her meyster þei shal mich trobull þ^{e} and if þow be not trobuled. with hem.' þ^{u} art fauerer of hir synnes. / A voise seid. fro heuen. to arseny. Arseny. flee men. and þow shalt be saued. / and eft it seid to hym. Fuge. tace. quiesce arseny fle. Be stil. and. duel stedfastly. in sum sted fro þe peple in sum rest // here. wil. sum men sey. þat for to write or speke. so mych of solitari lijf. amang þ^{e} comen peple of þe world / is bot foly. / For. why and all men were solitary.' þen shold no men be marchantes. plugh men. ny men of craft. and so sholde þe world. be confounded and at an end / To þ^{is} wil. I answer. a⟨s⟩ seynt Ierom answerd to an herityke. þat was called. vigilancius / þis herityke argued in a like. maner ageyn. virginite / If all men were maydenes.' þ^{is} world were at an ende. / And Ierom answered hym þus If all men were foles. as þow art qwere shold men fynd a wise man. For as þer ar bot few folk in comparison þat ar stired. to virginite.' So þer are bot few in comparison þat ar sti'red. to be solitari / And þerfor such argumentes if all men wer wilful pore. If all men or wymen were meydenes If alle men wer solitari.' þ^{is} world shold not be susteyned.' are vnwittyly spokyn. / For. vnnethes may any man or. woman be broght to such. maner of lyfyng / Neiþelese how al. men and wymmen shold in party be. solitary I wil sey afew wordys Seynt gregory 4 moralium opon

9 gode: o *altered from* u (*different hand?*). Nota *in margin*. B. 20 a⟨s⟩: and *with* nd *expuncted and* s *written above*. 23 Nota *in margin*. B; meydenes *crossed through and expuncted after second* were. 34 duplex populorum *in margin*. B.

þ[is] text Iob. 3. Edifican[t] sibi solitudines spekes of ij maner of peple. þer ar sum þat setten. most her hert to haue worldly. worship̄ worldly. riches and lust of her flesh. and þis maner of peple ar full. of veyn þoughtes as he þat settes his hert on pride.' þinkes þus wold I do and it wer in my power / I. wold. haue mych meynȝe to do me seruice / I wold. be rially areyed I. shold auaunse hym & hym If any mañ disesed me. I shold ouercom hym. I shold haue lowtynges & reuerense. / A. couetouse man þinkes þat he wold haue riches. how soeuer he cam by hem. with symony with vsury. with lesinges sleg'htys. and forswerynges // þe lechure þinkes how he myght bring his lust aboute. / he rekys not how many wemen. he. defile. he spekes of rybaudry he. dremes of vnclennes. and þus þ[is] wiked peple. ar neuer solitari. For þouȝ þey be by hem one. her mynd is full. of liknes of men. of wymmen. of go'lde. of siluer. of this and of þat þat þey are euer in gret prese & gret /| thong at þ[e] lest with hem self / An oþer peple þer is þat desiren no þing þat is in þis warld. bot as to be a mene. to. bl⟨r⟩yng þem to endles blis þey vsen gold. siluer. mete drinke. and sum wedlóke bot her intent is in all. þis to vse hem after. goddes lawe. and for no thyng to breke goddes commoundmentes For þouȝ þey haue. besines outeward. as gouernance of houshold cure of paryshens as. parsones haue gouernance. of contres. and cytees. as She'refes. Maires. and Baylees. ȝit her intent is euer set on þing to do right and lawe. of god. kepyng clene. her con'science and many atyme such men. when þey are by hem selue. þey examyn her conscience. and if þey fynd any þing amys.' þey amenden it by trew penance. / þus þey are solit'ary. in her intent settyng her hert on. on þing þat is on right'wisnes. and goddes plesance. wich ar alon. Dauid þouȝ he wer a kyng and had mych peple aboute hym.' ȝit he was þus solitary. Vnam pecij a domino hanc requiram. &c Psalmo 26 / One thing he seid I haue asked.

f. 138v

18 thong *sic for* throng. 20 bl⟨r⟩yng *sic*, r *interlined*. 32 on[1]: op *interlined before* o *with caret*. B.

of þe lord. and þat shal. I seke þat I. dwel in þe house. of þe lord all þe deys of my liif / lo þouȝ þis kyng had gret besines outward.· ȝit his hert was solitari set. onely on on þing vpward. and þat was end|les. blis / Þe desire of mich folke. is to conforme hem to þe multi|tude of þe. world. in clothing festyng In dalyance In byyng in sellyng. and in oþer worldly condicions be þe god be þey badde. more. lokyng what þe wold / preyses. þen wat god commoundes. which is ageyn þe doctrine of þe apostle. ro. 12. Nolite conformari huic seculo. þat is loke ȝe haue no wil to be like. þe world in vanite. and fleshly delites / Also exodi 23. þe scriptur seis Non sequeris turbam ad faciendum ma|lum. þow shalt not folowe þe peple. in doyng yuell A. tre þat standes nere a stret qwer is comyn passage. of mych peple. may bryng / forþe no frute bothe god. and ripe as. Criso|stom seis in inperfecto omelia 32. But and it shall bryng forþe gude frute. and ripe It most stand in closed gardyn. or far fro þe passage. of men. / On þe same maner a man þat wil. vse. þe comyn spech of men. as veyn sweryng wariyng ribaudy & such oþer and. be like þis ietteres. in her nise arey. In riot and in oþer folies. he may not þus gouerned. bryng god gud purposis or. god intentes to effecte. and gostly frute. But a man most in his wil. þouȝ pershaunce he may not with his body be fer fro such condicioned peple. and vse not such yuel iangil|yng neiþer sich wiked wirkyng and if so be þat he has ben. of such euell. condicions bifor tym. hym most besi hym to com oute of hem. by a litel and a litel &
f. 139 custom hym /| to god condicions so þat his gode condicions increse and his bade decrece. And þus may euery man if he will. be in sum maner solitari and fer fro synful
(M. 164) condicions of þe world / viij resons þer are why a man. schold fle þe comyn condicions of þe world þe First is sekyrnes. If a wod lion. ran in þe strete.· a wise man. Eight reasons for leaving the world: I. Safety.

7 y *written in space between* þe *and* god. 8 wold *sic.*
17 opere *interlined after* in *with caret.* B. 34 nota. 8. causas fugiendi mundanas condicione[s] *in margin.* B.

wold. fle to house. and shyd þ^{e} dore. // Oure aduersary þ^{e} fende. as seynt petre seis gose aboute as a roryng lyon to deuoure vs. And where. gos. he:' Certeyn in proud peple. In bakbiters. In lechours. and such oþer deueles. lymmes wich stiren. men to syne. with hir wiked wordes with her yuel dedis and yuel ensoumpules. of wich euyl. stirers. to synne þe world is full. And þerfore a sekyr wey is as litel. as a man may to cum amog suc̄h folke. //

II. The fragile nature of virginity.

þe secund reson is a man þat beris a preciose licor in a brethel vessel as is glas he wald. be war þat he cam in no th⟨r⟩ong / lest be. brake his vessel. Seynt poul seis 2. corinthiorum 4 habemus. thesaurum in vasis fictilibus. we haue tresur in brethel vesselles. / A. preciouse tresur is mey'denhod. / so is also clennes. of conscience. / A. brithel. vessel. is manes. flesh Bewar þerfor. þow þat wil kep̄ maydenhod. þat þow cum not in such company. wher þow may lightly. breke þ^{i} vessel. for be it ones. brokyn. wil. it neuer be hole ageyn as it was bifore. For aman. or woman lesing her. maydehod by. bodily. dede of lichery may þey neuer be restored to meydenhod ageyn. nomore þen a vessel. of a̧ glasse. and it be brokyn may be mad hole. ageyn. / And ȝit meydenhod may be lost in sum maner raþer þen a vessel. of glas. may. be broken. For glas brekes not bot if it be touched. But meydenhod may be. lest by ful. consent of wil̄l to fleshly dede.:' þouȝ. þ^{e} ded be neuer done. Ne⟨rþ⟩eles þis maner brekyng of maydenhod may be restored ageyn. and. be as hole. as. euer it was. þorow medi'cyn. of contricion an sothfast schryfte. as. it is preued in seynt Ioh̄n Ewangelist which willyng to wed a wyfe:' God called hym fro weddyng and so he. dwelled styl̄l meyden neuer (M. 166) þ^{e} vnholier / to whome / as clene meyden. crist in his passion. betoke his moder to kep̄ whic̄h was most clene virgyne. Virginem virgini commendauit / Be war also when þ^{u} comes in company þat þow les. not clennes of

2 1^{a} *in margin*. B. 9 2^{a} *in margin*. B. 11 th⟨r⟩ong: r *interlined with caret*; be *sic, for* he. 26 Ne⟨rþ⟩eles *altered from* Neueles. 30 and to haue *in margin marked for insertion after* wed.

conscience by flateryng / By confourmyng to worldly meñ in sum vnleful ṭịþunges. For. hard it is to come among worldly peple. But a man go wors awey.' þen he came. / as. it is hard to bere bawm̄ in a thyn glas. in a
f. 139v gret prese and spille nogh̄t þerof // Crist | seyd̀ to his aposteles. Iōḅ. 16. In mundo pressuram &c // þat is in þe world ȝe shal haue thronge. and disese and þerfore it is gode to drawe fro such. throng to crist þat is verrey pese // þe þrid skil. is. heuen. is right hiȝe. For þi to hem þat will reche. þerto it is lityl. inogh̄. to cast all þe. world vndur her fete. and so ençhaunce hem self / to heuen werd. Apocalypsis 12 / Seynt Ioh̄n seis vidi mulierem. &c þat is to sey I saw a woman clo'þed with þe sune. and mone. vndur hir fete. / þe mone þat is euer wexing / or. wanyng and neuer stedfast.' betokynes. worldly þinges þat are euer changyng as now riche now pore. now hole. now seke. al worldli þinges most be troden vndur fete. þat þow forfeite not ageyn. rightwisnes for no worldly þing / and þat þow haue more affeccioñ to thinke on god to speke of god. to serue god.' þen to thinke. or to speke of worldly. wynnyng / or. worldly worship̄ / and so be cloþed with þe sune. þat is with heuenly and vertuos lifyng // Þe fourt skil is prowes and III. To obtain heaven.

(M. 168) nobylnes. of a cristen soule. / lordes. ladies and men of gret kyn. ber not on hem. pakkes. ny. bagges. as beggers. done. / Al worldly. þing.' is bot beggery and þerfore. bere it not bounden to þe in þin affeccion.' But as þe apostle seis prima timothei 6. / Habentes alimenta. &c haue we. mete. drinke and clothing / hold. we vs peyd / For. as seynt Ierom seis in þe prologe. of þe. bible. / mete dry'nke and choth.' are riches. of cristen men And who þat holden ⟨hem⟩ payed of litel. and simple liuelod. neden But litel. dele. with þe world // þe fift reson is Noble men & wemen. makyn large relefe. / Who may make lager. relef þen. Petre and þe aposteles. diden þat IV. Renunciation of wealth shows nobility. V. Liberality.

9 3a *in margin.* B. 23 4a *in margin.* B; werþynis *interlined above* prowes *crossed through.* B. 31 choth *sic.* 32 hem *interlined.* 33 nota bene & optime *in margin.* B. 35 lager *sic, for* larger; 5a *in margin.* B.

forsoken. all þinges. an sued crist // Neiþeles. to forsake þe world as þe apos|teles. did:' is a ded of perfeccion / And þerfor not al men ar bounden. to þat maner of forsakyng þ^{e} world / Bot euery man þat wil. be saued. most forsake þe world on þ^{is} wise. þat he luf it not vnordinatly / þat is to mene þat he breke. not þ^{e} com-moundment of god. for no worldly lucre. ny for no. worldly. worship̄ / as þey done þat fo⟨r⟩swerne hem for to wynne monegħ / For. þ^{e} comyn custom̄ of world|ly men. is for. worldly. honur and temperal. lucre to flater to liȝe. veynly to. swere and who þat vses. not such

VI. Fellowship with Christ. condicions is fer fro. worldly maner // þe sext reson. is a man may not be. frend to worldly maneres boþe at ones. as. seynt Iam seis iacobi 4 Quicumque voluerit amicus esse seculi &c // worl|dly maneres. haue gret delite in veyn daliance to speke // | of / worldly worshipes. f. 140 and fleshly lustes where þey þat desiren to haue frenship̄ of god. and. famulierite of his blessednes. lufen to take of goddes godnes. of þe gret kyndnes. þat he haues shewed. to man and of þ^{e} gret ioy. þat he haþe o⟨r⟩deyned for. man and such men. luuen. riches. welfare. in þ^{e} worlde / & fauour of worldly. men. in as mycħ as. þey are necessari to þ^{is} wreched. life. as. a tilman. loues. duunge. in as mycħ as it is necessari to. his lande // þe

VII. To see God. seuened / reson is clernes / of consciens. and. clennes. of hert qwicħ aman. may liȝtlier / come. by. þat haþe. litel (M. 170) to do with þe world / þan a noþer man þat haþe. mycħ to do with þ^{e} world / For gret besines. of þ^{e} world askes gret trubules. & many as oure lord. seid to Martha. luce 10 Martha martha solicita es. &c / As. in a standing water þat is clere a man may. wele se. his face. wicħ þing he may not do and þ^{e} water be trobeled / So a man trobled with worldly besines:' may not se. þe state of his con-science. so clerly as he shold do. if he fled. sucħ worldly

6 vnordinatly: vn *separated from rest of word by interrupted vertical line.* 8 fo⟨r⟩swerne: r *interlined with stroke.* 12 6^{a} *in margin.* B. 13 an to god *marked by caret after* maneres, *and written in bottom margin.* B. 20 o⟨r⟩deyned: r. *interlined with stroke.* 25 7^{a} *in margin.* B.

besines and labored aboute rest of soule. // þe eg⟨h⟩t VIII. reson is þ^{is}. Men confourmyng hem self to comyn. con= dicions of þe world / ocupyen hir outward wittes aboute sicħ þinges as þ^{e} warld / has most delite in. qwer men þat setten. litel. by þ^{e} world:' full warly. kepen her vtter wittes as. is bifore diffusly wretyñ in þe first parte. of þis tretys. / For vnwar kepyng of þ^{e} vtter wittes:' is cause of gederyng of many wiked þo'ughtes. in þe. hert / It is red. 3. regum 2 þat kyng Salomon. com'mounded to semey. which had ben a wiked mañ and charged. hym opeyn of detħ þat he shold bilde hym an house. in (M. 172) Ierusalem. and duel. þer / And if he passid out / of þe cite:' he shold be sleyn. / þis simei þat had deserued deth and hade asked forgifnes. was ful feyn of þ^{is} couenant and assented þerto / þen Simey duelled in ierusalem many d⟨a⟩es But it befel þre. ȝere after þat his seruantes flowen fro hym oute of Ierusalem Symey also passed oute of Ierusalem. and sued after hem. fo⟨r⟩ whicħ ded. ageyn his couenant Salomon made. to sle hym. / By þ^{is} yuil man Simei:' may be vnderstonden. ylk synful man wich. has. deserued endles detħ wich is sory for his synnes. and askes god fo⟨r⟩gif'nes. as. Simei asked þ^{e} kynge. God þat is most gracyouse forg'yffes. such aman. his synne vnder þis condicion þat he make hym a gostly habitacion within his oune soul. which is vn'derstanden. by Ierusalem þat is as mych to sey as sigħt of pese. þis is þus mycħ to mene þat a man shold entre oft in | f. 140v to his soul. by wise consideracions and stedfast belefe. and se how he was. ordyned. if he wil lif cristenly to haue endles pese and kep̄ hym selfe fro remorse. of con= science so þat he kep̄ inw'ard pese. bituix þ^{e} citeȝines of his soul. þat are mynd vnderstan'ding reson. & wele insoumple. / þow. knowest by þ^{i} mynde. þat þow. hast lerned þat þ^{u} sholdest not liȝe ny forswer þe. neiþer bigyle no man. for. no worldly couetiȝe. þat þ^{u} shold do

1 8^{a} *in margin*. B; eg⟨h⟩t: h *interlined, with stroke*. 16 d⟨a⟩es: a *interlined*. 18 fo⟨r⟩: r *interlined, with stroke*. 29 ymaginacion *in margin*. 31 sensus interiores *in margin*. B.

no lichery and þus oþer synnes. þu knowest wele and vnder|standest / by reson þat þow shold do no such dedis as god·has. forbed. / þus þi mynd þin vnderstand-yng and þi resoun are at gode acorde. in þi soule and if þi will. acord with hem þat þow wil not do such euil. dedis bot kepist þe fro hem.' þen findest þow agostly pese within þi selfe Wherfor such a soul. may wel be caled. Ierusalem. þat is to sey siȝte of pes / Bot and þi wil be contrary to mynd. and reson þat þow. w⟨i⟩l liȝe. forswere. bigile or. do. lecheri.' þen is not þi soul Ieru-salem. for pese is not in þi soule // Many men kepyn such. gostly pes for. a tyme. But allas þe seruantes of þe soule. þe which are þer v. outwarde. wittes sum tym passen fro þe gouernanse of reson. as þe sight in behold-yng vanitees. þe eer. in heryng of vanitees and þus of oþer wittes. and þen a man is so temped to such vanitees þat oft tyme he folowes his fl|eshly stirynges and gose in a maner fro hym selfe foȝetyng þe god acord. of mynd. vnderstandyng and reson þat was in his soule. and falles. into lechiry. into appetite of wor|ship ageyn right into enmyte of certeyn persones. for þinges þat he herys. and sees. And what foloues. of þis But riȝt as. Simei was. sleyn. at þe biddyng of salomon. for he keped not þe couenaunt and þe termes. þat þe kyng had ly|met vnto hym.' So such a man. þat kepis not his lifyng within þe termes of goddes law. is sleyn gostly for. god þat is lijf of þe soule. is partied. þerfro þorow dedly synne. For als mych þen. as it is so. perilouse to hem. þat wold lif go stly. þat her wittes be so besied. owtward.' holsum it wer / to luke mych inward. and as clerkes redyn. in bokes of sci|ence. for to gete conyng / So þat such folke rede oft in þe bookes of her consciences. to get þerby gode leuyng / of þe bokes of conscience. spekes þe scripture. danielis 7. & apocalypsis 20 libri aperti sunt / þat is to sey. bokys. are opyned þe menyng of holy. writ is þis þat at þe last iugement þe bokes of all menes

1 of *interlined, with stroke after* þus. 9 w⟨i⟩l: i *interlined, with caret.* 13 nota *in margin*. B. 18 foȝetyng *sic.*

consciense. shal be opinly knowen to al men and after such þinges as is wretyn. in her conscience. so shal þey be demed Loke forþ^{i} þat þ^{e} boke of þ^{i} conscience be f. 141 wele & trewly wetyn | A boke þat sholde be. wel and profetably wretyn. neded to be. wele r⟨e⟩uled þe. bokes of many mens. conscience. are ful. euyl. reuled. for. sum haue. to brod conscience. Sum to narow and to streyte. and sum haue corruped consciences prima timothei 4 cauteriatam habencium conschenciam // To brod consciences haue þey wich char'gen no sinnes But sich as. þe world. wondris on as men qwellyng auouteri. and robry. // For of veyn sweryng of lesynges: to kep men. fro harme of to mych or to oft etyng and. drinkyng of veyne Iangyllyng and such oþer haue þey no conscience. But þ^{e} scripture seis ecclesiastici 19 Qui spernit mo'dica paulatim decidet / he þat despises. smal synnes. shal. bilitel and by litel. fall. into grete synnes. as he þat vses co'mynly. veyn sweryng. falles of into forsweryng whe'rfore. crist matthei 5 wil þat men withstand þ^{e} first brunt of synnes as. vnskilful. wrathe. to þ^{i} Broþer Beholdyng of wymmen to desire hem. vnlefully veyn sweryng / and such oþer For þat withstondes þe first temptacion of wrath.' shall not fall into manqwellyng / he þat withstandes lecherous lokes and consentyng to lechery. shal not fal into þ^{e} ded of lechery. / And þus a man to kep hym fro veyn sweryng kepis hym fro forsweryng / Iudith þe holi wedow. kyt of þ^{e} hed of Olefernes. prince. of goddes enmyes. And so was he and al his host ouercommen. Iudith 13° // þus kytt of þ^{e} hedys. of dedly synnes. þat is to sey withstand þ^{e} first be'ginyng when þ^{u} art stired to synne and þen shalt þow withstand yuil. dedes. and euil. wordes þat suen consentyng to synne and so shalt þow. ouercom al. þ^{e} host of wikednes. / wiked wedes wold be destried. wiles ye be ȝonge. and sekneses heled in her begynnyng // To streit conscience

4 wetyn *sic*. 5 r⟨e⟩uled: e *interlined with stroke*. 9 Nimis larga conscienc[ia] *in margin*. B. 35 stricsta consciencia *in margin*. B.

haue þey wych demen ich euyl. þought synne. As if þoughtes com ageyn þ^{e} beleue or ageyn þ^{e} worship of god or oure lady or / of despeir or any oþer such heuy þoughtes and þow consentes not to hem or on sum þat haue such þougthes wynnen þey synen bot / it is not so. / Sentis non consentis seis seynt Bernard to mene If þow haue any such heuy þoughtes and þow consentes not hem. þow felest temptacion Bot þ^{u} synnest not // If a lecheurus man stired a chast woman. to vnclennes and she heryng hym were displesed with his talkyng. she syned neuer a dele / So when þ^{e} fend or þ^{i} fleshe stires þ^{e} to any synne be it neuer so gret or neuer so foule if þow consentist not þ^{u} sinest not / A man may not lett a brid to fle þorow his house.' But he may let hym þat | he shal. nestil. in his house. So. I may not let a foule f. 141^{v} þought to. passe. þorow my. soule. But I may. withstand it þat if it file not my soul. by consentyng þerto. / wherfore. our lord seis to his peple. ysaie primo auferte. malum. cogitacionum vestrarum ab oculis meis take ȝe. awey. þe. yuil. of ȝoure þoughtes fro myn. eghen. he. seis not take. ȝe. awey. ȝour euil. þoghtes fro myn eghen for. no man can defend þat he shal haue non euyl. þoghtes But he may so gouerne. hym. þorow goddes. grace þat he shall not consent. to wiked thoghtes wich consentyng is þ^{e} euyl. of þ^{e} þoght of which wordes sues. þat conscience þat demes iche. euyl þoght synne is to streit // Corruped conscience haue þey. which chargen. more. synes. done ageyn man þen ag'eyn god. / holi writ seis primo regum 2. Si peccauerit. vir in virum &c Si autem in dominum &c / þat is to mene If aman trespase. ageyn a man. ȝit god may be plesed by prayers. and sacrifises But and a man synne ageyn. god. god. who shal. prey. for. hym.' / .As. Who sey. It is mych more. greuouse. to synne ageyn god. immediatly. þen ageyn

5 wynnen: *sic for* wynen. MS. wymen *with first minim expuncted.* 6 to, *standing at line-end altered to* þ^{t}, *and* is to mene *added in margin, all in different hand.* 13 nota *in margin.* B. 19 nota *in margin.* B. 22 hym *in margin marked to follow* defend. 27 corrupta consciencia *in margin.* B. 32 god. god. *sic.*

man immedyatly. En'soumple. / It is a gretter synne to aman. to. forsuere hym wi'lfully. þen to wound a man. wilfully. If a man smete þ^{e} kyng with vialence. a litel. stroke.' he shold be ponyshed more. for. for. þat litel. stroke. þen if he. wounded a ȝoman ful. sore / þus all þ^{e} synes þat ben ageyne þ^{e} reuerence. of god'dis mage⸗state. as mawmetry willfull. forsweryng wich'craft & sych oþer are. passyng synnes. and gret / Thre. þinges. shold. aman charge in his conscience. First and princi'paly þ^{e} commoundmentes. of god / þen commoundmentes of ho'ly chirch / and þen. his awne deuocions and his own̄. vowes. But many men chargen more her owne de'uocions.' þen þe ordinaunce of holy chirch For þey haue more. deuocion to sey. a preier. an oryson. of her owne takyng and her owne list þen to sey matynes houres. or euensong. ȝ⟨h⟩e þouȝe þey bounden. þerto by ordur of profession or. to sey þe pater noster þat god he. selfe. ordeyned þey haue more. likyng to fast a. wedenesday of her own takyng.' þen to fast þe ymbre dayes and vigiles of seyntes as. holy chirch has ordeyned and more con'science. haue þey if þey breke her. owne deuocions or her owne vowes. þen if þey breke. þ^{e} commoundmentes of god. or. of holi
f. 142 chi⟨r⟩che. Sum ordered men haue more // | conscience. if þei take. a. respond or a. versicle. oþer þen þey shuld sey.' þen if þey make. a. wilful lesyng in excusacion̄ of hem selfe / or swere. by goddes body vnreuerently. // Sum vnlerned. peple haue. more. conscience. sum dey. þat þey here mo masse..' þen þogh þey bigyle. her neght⸗bure. notably or. þoȝe forswere hem. self in marchandise / Also þ^{e} conscience. of such men is corrupud which chargen more smale sines þen gretter. as. sum men. haue more. conscience to ete. ij morsell of bred on a fasting day / þen þoȝe þey dranke. a potel. ale. or. wyne. whoso. þerfor wil haue a wele ruled conscience..' let him haue. conscience of ich synne. But gretter conscience of gretter synnes. /

15 ȝ⟨h⟩e: h *interlined; a small curved mark after* e *is perhaps intended as punctuation.* 23 chi⟨r⟩che: r *interlined.* 24 nota *in margin.* B.

And hym most principally. and most charge. þe commoundmentes of god for. þo ben. vndispensable. of any man. in erthe þe pope may not dispense with me. ny gif me lefe. to swere. veynly to make lesynges or to be a lechoure. þen shal he haue next in worshiþ þe commoundmentes of holi chirch as to fast vi'giles of seyntes and also he most keþ his owne. vo⟨w⟩se if þey. be descretly made. Neiþeles preceptes of þe chirch and vowes. wilfully made. may in many a cace be despensed with of prelates þat haue. powere. If þe buke of þi conscience be. þus reuled / þen is wele. þen luke. þe lefes of þis buke are mynd. vnderstandyng an wil. And wonder not þouȝe. I cal. hem leeues. wich I caled. byfore citeȝynse ọṛ lẹụẹṣ. For as crist is caled. hostium ouium & pastor / Ioannis 10 dore. of þe folde. and þe shepherd / Also after diuerse consideracions.ᐟ So may Mynd. vnderstandyng / and. wil. be called citeȝinese. or leues. after diuerse consideracions. Rede þen in þe lefe of þi mynde. if þow. haue ben Prowd. and presumptuose. a lechur / a lesingmonger / . a begiler a slugard /. wheþer þu haue forsw'orne þe. or. detrated þin euen cristen. Red þe godnes and þe kyndnes. þat god. has. shewed. to þe. and how vnkynd þu hast ben ageyn. Prei god þen þat þu may haue a knyfe. of sherþ contricion and rase awey þe foule lustes and likynges of synnes. bifor. done. And þen write in þi mynd þe abhomin'acion of þi sines and how þu hast deserued. to be euer in hel. fire. and neuer to com in blis how þu hast offended. god fal'sly. and treiterously and sey with kyng Eȝechi isaie 38 Reco'gitabo tibi omnes annos. meos. in amaritudine &c / þat is to sey I shal remembre me. of al my ȝeres. how I haue di[sp]le'sed þe lord. and þerfore. wil I suffer / bitter contricion i[n] my soule. write in þi mynd how mankynd is infeked. by | þe fall of þe first man. and woman how. gret trauel. f. 142v

7 vo⟨w⟩se: w *written above* i *expuncted.* 9 nota *in margin.* B. 12 þat þey be treuly wretin þe lefes of þis boke *written in margin and marked to be inserted after* buke. 20 nota bene *in margin.* B. 21 detrated *sic.* 31–32 *MS. damaged.*

& peyne. men. haue. to gete her bodili. liuelod how moderes bringen forþe. hire chyldren. with mych pyne. and sorowe. how in þ^{e} tyme. of noee þ^{is} warld was nyȝe. distrewed for synne how it shal be. destrewed. at þ^{e} last by a flode of fire how it behoued. crist god and man to diȝe most shamfull deth to make a seth for. man synne qwate sorowes whate sekneses. qwat penance men don̄ and sufferen for. her synn shuch remembrance. shuld gender. dred in a manes. soule. and stir hym to do trew penance for his synnes bifor don̄ & make. hym a ferde to fall to syn ageyn. But lest a man for. to mych dred fel into wanhop. he shold. writ in his mynd. how mercyful god is in forgifyng of synne / how. he receyued to grace synnful mary Magdeleyn. Petre þat for'soke. crist and forsware hym falsly. Paul þat pursued cristes chirch / þ^{e} thef also þat was. hanged. with hym / think how. þ^{e} lord by his prophet eȝechielis .18. behetys vs. grace and remissi'on. of oure synnes. what tyme or houre þat we trewly conuerted. such þoughtes shal. kep̄ vs. in hop̄ / low what þ^{e} wyse man seis ecclesiastici 11. In die bonorum immemor ne sis malorum & in die malorum ne immemor. sis bonorum / þat is in þ^{e} day of gode þinges. be not myndles. of yuel þinges / And in þ^{e} day of yuel. þinges be not myndeles of gode þinges þat is to mene. when þ^{u} art in þ^{i} propsperite and art stired þorow. godis þat god has gyuen þe. to pride. to presumpcion. or to any wantonnes.: Bethinke þ^{e} of þ^{i} wiked. synnes. and w'hat euil peynes þow. hast deserued for. hem and þat þow shal. kep̄ þ^{e} in dred / on þat oþer side. when þ^{u} art in aduersite and hast gret heuynes.: Beþinke þ^{e} of goddes godnes what luf he has shewed to þ^{e} þen. bryng to mynd þ^{i} gode dedis to strengh þ^{i} selfe in hop̄ and þus þorow þ^{e} grace of god shal þ^{u} be keped fro presumpsion and. wanhop̄. When þ^{u} has þus. red in þ^{e} lefe of þi mynd: red þen in þ^{e} lefe of þin vnderstanding what knowyng þow. hast wheþer þ^{u} know verely vice fro vertu. Wheþer

3 nota intime *in margin*. B. 25 nota de prudentia *in margin*; propsperite *sic*.

þ^{u} know. wic̄h is gretter synne. which is lesse synn. Our first moder Eue supposed ⟨at⟩ þ^{e} stiryng of þ^{e} fende þat it had ben no sinne to haue etyn of þe appyll. Adam wist wel it was syn. But he wend it had not ben so grete syn as it was. þe lefes. of her vnderstandyng were. not wele wretyn. þus. if þ^{u} wene. þat it be no syn to swere veynly or to liȝe to saue þ^{i}selfe. fro bodily harme If þ^{u} deme forsweryng or fornicacion to be bot litel syn.' þe lef of þin vnderstandyng is miswretyn. | Boicius seis in his f. 143 topikes. / Malum non potest vitari nisi cognitum. Aman may not fle. yuil. bot if he knowe. it / loke qweþer þ^{u} can rehers þ^{e} ten commoundmentes. and if þ^{u} can rehers. hem.' luke if wheþer þow canst do hem./ Red in þ^{i}se⟨l⟩fe wheþer þu can paciently su'ffre aduersitees. as. wronges Pouert and seknes. wheþer þow haue any. ruthe of peple. þat are in disese. and. wheþer þow may fynd. in þ^{i} hert gladli to help̄ hem. after þ^{i} pouere / If þ^{u} can not do þus. lerne. to know. and lerne. to life. wele. And sey with Dauid Psalmo. 118. Da mihi intellectum ut discam mandata tua / Lord gif me. vnderstandyng þat I lerne þi commoundmentes dauid co'wth. rehers. þ^{e} ten commoundmentes. But he prayed to god gif hym conyng to do hem. wele. and. better and. better // Rede þen in þ^{e} þrid lefe. of þis boke þat is þi wil / loke what desire þ^{u} hast to be trew. to be clene. lifer / oute. of lechiri wheþer þ^{u} haue more. ioy to speke and here. of god. and. heuenly lifyng.' þen to speke or. here of worldly. wynnyng / . or veyn tales. / loke how redi we ben. to. euyl. and how dulle to godnes & deuocion If þis lefe. of þe. wil. shold be. wele wretin / a man nedis to aske þre. þinges. of god þat þ^{e} wil be agode. wil. a right̄ wil and. a ful. wil / prey god þat þ^{i} wil be. so gode. þat þ^{u} consent not to wikednes. But to such þinges as. ben profetable. to þ^{i} body and to þ^{i} soule. Also þat þi. wil be right̄ / þat al þat euer þ^{u} purposes. spekes. or. does. þat it be for a gode ende. not for veyn glory not principally for

2 at *interlined, with stroke.* 13 þ^{i} se⟨l⟩fe: l *interlined, with stroke.*

worldli lucre or fauour of men But to go'ddes. worship̄ principalli and þi gostly. profet Also þat þ^{i} wil be. ful þat þ^{u} lese not þi gode will and þi gode dedis for no dred of man. neþer for. worldly shame. þis iij lefes. Mynd vnder'standyng and. wil / wold. of⟨t⟩ be examened We reden eȝechielis primo þat þe prophet eȝechiel siȝe iiij bestes. and ich̄ on of þ^{e} iiij bestes had iiij faces. þ^{e} face of a man þ^{e} face of a lyon / þe face of an oxe. and þe. face of an egle. And ich on of þes. bestes. went by fore. his owne face. & þey turned not ageyn. when þey. wente. // Neiþeles. soñ after he. seis þey went and turned ageyne. / Bi þes. beestes as seynt Gregori seis omelia 4 super eȝechiele / may be. vnderstanden ich gode cristen man. or. creatur / wich̄ sho'ld. haue a mannes. face. in gouernyng hym self after reson þat he liif not beestly. he shold haue a lyons face. in myghty withstanding of syn / he. shold. haue as an ox or a calues face. in sacrifiyng hym self bi trew. penance for. syn byfor. doñ For. of calues. was sacrifice made. in þ^{e} old law to god and he shold. haue as. an egiles face. in beholdyng heuenly þinges as. what ioy and. blis is ordeyned to gode lifers þis iiij bestes went by fore her owne faces. A man f. 143^{v} walkys / | gostly bifor his owne. face. When he. takes hede of his þoghtes. of his wordes. of his dedys. and if þey be euil he avoydis hem not consentyng to yuel þoghtes and doyng penance fo⟨r⟩ euil. wordes. and dedis kepyng hym self. afterward fro al wikednes. in his wil and if he conceyue þat his purposes. are gode. and acordyng to his degre. he has. desire to fulfill hem / he lufes to speke. vertuosly. and do profetably. A man þat more. takes hed of oþer menes. synnes þen of his owne.' is like to aman þat lokes not his owne fete. bot fer fro hym and so he may ligħtly cach̄ a fall. and be hurted. // A man þat takes. no hede to his foule. & euil þoghtes. bot lettes hem alon. and he þat can not kep̄ cilence.

5 of⟨t⟩: t *interlined, with stroke.* 26 r *interlined.* 30 nota optima *in margin.* B. 32 to *in margin marked for insertion after* not. B.

Bot iangiles of vanite. and of þing vnprofetable. and he þat rekes. not what he. dose. / Such folke walken not byfor her owne. face. For. þey se not wel þem self // þes. bestes wal'ked and. turned not ageyn for. ich man. and woman of ȝeres of discrecion shold besy hem. to leue yuel condicions & to encrece in godnes. þat as. þey. wex in age:' So þey be better / and better and not to turne ageyn. wilfully to yuil maneres þat þey haue forsaken. / Nerþelese. for. it ⟨is⟩ seid byfore. þes bestes went and turned not ageyn. and also þey went and turned ageyn. / þerfore. it is to witt þat a man shal go fro vice to vertew as fro falshed. to treuþe. fro lechery to chastite and þus of oþer and not turne ageyn. to vices / But a man þat goes. fro als gode. dede to a more gode dede.:' most oft tyme. turne ageyn. as. it is a gode dede a tilman or a crafty man to do his labour. treuly. It is a better dede to here. amesse. or. a sermon and ȝit most such a man go fro þe messe. heryng or. fro þe sermon to his occupacion ageyn. And þus most prelates. and folke of religion go oft tyme fro dedis of contemplacion as. redyng and preyng:' to actiue dedis for her owne nede. and for. profet of oþer men. as to prech to viset þe pore. also to ete and drinke wich are gode. dedis if þei be done. for agode hende. / þus þen keping warly þi v. outward wittes as it is wreten in þe first party of þis tretis and examynyng þi selfe & keping þi self inward as þow art taght in þis secund party:' þow shall wele kep þe wordes. of Salomon with which þis simple tretis begynes. Omni custodia serua cor. tuum &c with al warde kep þin hert &c.

9 is *interlined with caret.*
Lichfeild tractatus de V. sensibus explicit *added at end.* L.

The manufacturer's authorised representative in the EU for product safety is Oxford University Press España S.A. of El Parque Empresarial San Fernando de Henares, Avenida de Castilla, 2 - 28830 Madrid (www.oup.es/en or product.safety@oup.com). OUP España S.A. also acts as importer into Spain of products made by the manufacturer.

Printed and bound by CPI Group (UK) Ltd, Croydon, CR0 4YY

20/03/2026

02075339-0003